Bread for the Journey

Resources for Worship

Edited by Ruth C. Duck

The Pilgrim Press
New York

Acknowledgments

Special thanks are due to all who contributed materials to this book and to the faith communities that inspired them. The author of each section is identified by initials. Contributors are:

Charles Bagby (CB)	Mary Sue Gast (MSG)
Michael Bausch (MB)	Dennis Knight (DK)
Lavon Bayler (LB)	William George Myers, O.S.L. (WGM)
Ruth C. Duck (RCD)	Mary Ann Neevel (MAN)
Mitzi Eilts (ME)	Marilee Scroggs (MS)
Keith Farnham (KF)	Mary Jo Stirling (MJS)
Paul J. Flucke (PJF)	Roger Straw (RS)
Wheadon United Methodist Church Worship Commission, Evanston, Illinois (WUMC)	William R. Wolfe (WRW)

Thanks go also to the Ecumenical Women's Center for help in gathering these materials.

No part of this publication may be reproduced, stored in a retrieval system, or transmitted in any form or by any means, electronic, mechanical, photocopying, recording, or otherwise (brief quotations used in magazines or newspaper reviews excepted), without the prior permission of the publisher. However, permission is hereby granted to churches to reprint material for use in worship services, provided that it is not reprinted from other publications (RSV and KJV excepted; see below and pages 95-96), and provided that the following notice is included: Reprinted by permission of the publisher from *Bread for the Journey,* ed. Ruth C. Duck. Copyright © 1981 The Pilgrim Press.

Unless otherwise indicated all biblical quotations and paraphrases are from the *Revised Standard Version of the Bible,* copyright 1946, 1952 and © 1971 by the Division of Christian Education, National Council of Churches, and are used by permission. Scripture quotations identified as TEV are from *Good News Bible,* Today's English Version, © American Bible Society, 1966, 1971, 1976. Used by permission. Those identified as KJV are from the *King James Version of the Bible.* PHILLIPS material is from the Revised Edition of *The New Testament in Modern English* translated by J.B. Phillips and is adapted with permission of Macmillan Publishing Company, Inc. and William Collins, Sons & Co., Ltd., © J.B. Phillips 1958, 1960, 1972. The lines of poetry in the Introduction are from *The Sorrow Dance* by Denise Levertov. Copyright © 1966 by Denise Levertov. Reprinted by permission of New Directions Publishing Corporation.

Library of Congress Cataloging in Publication Data
Main entry under title:

Bread for the journey.

Includes bibliographical references.
1. Worship programs, I. Duck, Ruth C., 1947-
BV198.B68   264   81-5046
ISBN 0-8298-0423-4 (pbk.) AACR2

3d printing, 1984

The Pilgrim Press, 132 West 31 Street, New York, New York 10001

Contents

INTRODUCTION

The image of life as a journey is another way of saying that faith and worship grow out of our stories and the story of God's people moving through time. This approach to faith and worship assumes that the experiences out of which they grow are important.

A group of us who had been part of Grailville Women in Ministry Week in 1977 were organizing a first national meeting of United Church of Christ clergywomen, to be held in January 1979. We were sitting in my dining room eating chili when I mentioned in passing that I had been writing many of my own worship resources in a desire to use language that includes both the masculine and the feminine in humanity and in God-imagery, and to draw on scripture images from the three-year ecumenical lectionary (appointed texts for every Sunday). The women all but cheered when I said I'd thought of organizing materials for publication, for they too felt the need for a greater variety of inclusive resources. *Sisters and Brothers Sing* (1977) by Sharon and Tom Neufer Emswiler and *Worship: Inclusive Language Resources* (1977) by the United Church of Christ Office for Church Life and Leadership offered some excellent resources, but we wanted more.

In the summer of 1978 I took our idea to the Grailville Women in Ministry Week and looked for people to help with the project. A group met to discuss what might be included in our book, and we enlisted the support of the Chicago Ecumenical Women's Center and its current coordinator, Sally Dries. The center ran a notice asking for materials, and much of the material in this book came from that appeal. After the initial planning process, I edited this book, with support and advice from Mary Ann Neevel and Michael Bausch, two Wisconsin clergy colleagues. Hazel Staats, secretary of Bethel-Bethany United Church of Christ, Milwaukee, of which I am pastor, graciously found spare time to type the manuscript, to the neglect of her garden and grandchild.

The companion volume to this book is *Everflowing Streams: Songs for Worship*, edited by Michael Bausch and Ruth C. Duck. Reflecting the same concern for inclusive language and for justice and peace, it includes adaptations of familiar hymns and singable new songs by such people as Carole Etzler, Tom Hunter, Jim Manley, Steve Rose, Susan Savell, Jim Strathdee, and Ruth Duck.

All the materials in *Bread for the Journey* come out of the lives of specific congregations and faith communities. They represent our faith and worship in process, always on a journey never complete. The dream born over chili will be realized only if these resources spark your own creativity and reflection in regard to the use of language and imagery to reflect our experience as Christian people on a journey at this point in history.

The title was suggested by images from a poem and from scripture. In "Stepping Westward," poet Denise Levertov speaks of the poles of feminine experience: to be constant, but also to move with life's seasons, "glad to be what, woman, and who myself, I am . . . " She closes with this image:

. . . If I bear burdens

they begin to be remembered
as gifts, goods, a basket

of bread that hurts
my shoulders but closes me

in fragrance. I can
eat as I go.

From scripture one is reminded of the manna from heaven, which fed the Exodus sojourners in the wilderness. At this time in the life of the church, there are burdens to be borne and struggles to be endured for the sake of justice and peace and the wholeness that comes from incorporating all sorts of people into our life. At times—and perhaps particularly when we struggle to change sacred words—it seems as if we are stealing holy bread from the tabernacle. Yet we have a journey that is ours to follow in this season of the church's life. The bread that sustains us is the presence of the Spirit and of the others who travel with us, and the stories of God's journey with the faithful throughout time. May this bread sustain you as you seek the path of faithfulness for your here and now.

Mile-Markers: Resources for the Sacraments and Rites of the Church

Baptism Liturgies

A Celebration of Baptism

Opening Words

LEADER: Baptism is a moment in the Christian community when we recognize the grace of God living in each newborn creation. God offers us the possibility of transformation, a continuing process of renewal of body, mind, and spirit, which takes place within faith communities. So it is that (parent/s) and all (child)'s family bring (her/him) into this community to be baptized.

Parent/s, child, family, and close friends draw together in a circle with the leader.

Congregational Reading

The community affirms its faith using a statement of faith, words of a hymn, or song special to the community. Be sure to use inclusive language.

Pledges to God and to One Another

LEADER: A covenant is integral to relationships with God, so today we state the responsibilities of parents and community to God and the child. (Parents' first names), I ask you now to affirm your covenant with God and with your child.

PARENTS*: We acknowledge our child's need for nurture in a Christian community of caring and concerned people, that (s/he) may explore the dynamics of a God who created and loves (her/him).

We covenant to bring (her/him) into the life of the Christian community to worship, to hear the story of the roots of our faith, to be called into response to the gospel, and to be in relationship with other believers as (s/he) grows into (her/his) own choice of faith in God.

LEADER: (Godparents' names), I ask you now to affirm your covenant with God, these parents, and this child.

GODPARENTS: Recognizing that there are many persons who touch the lives of children beyond their parents, we covenant to give our time and ourselves to this child, providing (her/him) with further opportunities to explore (her/his) growing experience of God and self. We will share our faith lifestyle with (her/him).

---

* When possible, parents may write their own pledge.

LEADER: Now I ask this congregation, what will be your part in helping this child discover the grace of God within (her/himself)?

CONGREGATION: We promise to give these parents our support as they live with this child in the pathways of Christ. We offer ourselves also, as ones who take (child) into our love, our prayers, and our daily lives, striving to build a community rich in the Spirit of God in which to nurture (her/him).

The Waters of Baptism

LEADER: Baptism is an act of naming and knowing one's identity, within the community and individually before God. Baptism is a recommitment of a creation with its Creator. Baptism is a bond of love. Let us pray.

God, your grace has been with (child) ever since you communed with (parent/s) in (her/his) creation. Be with (her/him) even now and with us (her/his) faith community, through the years, blessing (her/his) life, that (s/he) may grow in love for you. Amen.

(Parent/s), by what name shall this child of God be known?

PARENT/S: (Child's name.)

LEADER: We baptize you in the name of the Creator, Sustainer, and Redeemer.

Prayers and Blessings

The people gathered are invited to share their prayers and blessings with parent/s and child, verbally or physically, in the form of hugs, laying on of hands, smiles, etc.

Benediction

LEADER: Come with me, with us, into the soul of creation. The waters have opened and flow even now. New life is ahead!

(ME)

The Sacrament of Baptism

PASTOR: The sacrament of baptism symbolizes the love by which God reaches out to us even when we are very young. We are here today to declare that God loves (child) and to offer ourselves as the instruments of that love in (her/his) life.

PARENTS (AND SPONSORS): Because of God's love shown to us in Jesus Christ and the life of celebration this love brings, we want to have (child) baptized into the life and faith of this community. We ask God's guidance in helping (child) to grow to respect (him/herself) and others. We bring (him/her) here today with joy, accepting the trust that has blessed us with (his/her) life.

BROTHERS AND SISTERS: We are grateful for (child)'s coming into our family, and we want to share with (him/her) the love and faith that have been given to us.

7

CONGREGATION: We, as a community, promise to care for (child) by our actions and style of life. We will teach (him/her) the joys of God's world. We will love (him/her). We are by this affirmation inseparably bound with (him/her).

DEACON: On behalf of the congregation I say to you, (parent/s names), that (child's name) has with us here a community that is filled with love for (him/her), our homes are (his/her) homes, our resources are (his/her) resources. Our faith will be taught to (him/her). We pray that we might fulfill our vows to you and to God.

PASTOR: Let us pray. God, our Creator, we thank you for your faithfulness promised in this sacrament, and for the hope we have in Jesus Christ. As we baptize with water, baptize us with the Holy Spirit, so that what we say may be your word, and what we do may be your work. By your power, may we be made one with Jesus Christ in common faith and purpose. Amen.

(Child's name), I baptize you in the name of God the Creator, Jesus Christ the Redeemer, and the Holy Spirit who sustains us. Amen.

This child is now received into the love and care of the church. See what love God has given us that we should be called children of God; and we are!

Let us pray. Almighty God, giver of life, you have called us by name and pledged to each of us your faithful love. We pray for your child (name). Watch over (him/her). Guide (him/her) as (he/she) grows in faith. Give (him/her) understanding, and a quick concern for neighbors. Help (him/her) to be a true disciple of Jesus Christ, who was baptized your child and servant and who is our risen Head.

God of grace, we pray for (child)'s parent/s, (name/s). Help them to know you, to love with your love, to teach your truth, and to tell the story of Jesus to this child, so that (child) may hear your word and know of your presence. Amen.

ALL: Gracious God, giver of life, you have called us by name, and pledge to each of us your faithful love. We pray today for your blessing on (child), that you will watch over (him/her) and guide (him/her) as (he/she) grows in faith. Remind us of the promises of our own baptism, and renew our trust in you. Make us strong to obey your will and to serve you with joy, through the power of the Holy Spirit. Amen.

(MAN/PJF)

NOTE: This service is a composite of several services, planned by Mary Ann Neevel and Paul Flucke (ministers of Plymouth United Church of Christ, Milwaukee), drawing on the faith expression of the parents.

Communion Liturgies

A Service of Communion and Covenant Renewal to Celebrate the New Year

The Confession

LITURGIST: Looking at the year behind us, let us confess our inadequacy in living up to our high calling as sons and daughters of God.

ALL: O God, we know that we are a wayward people. Our footsteps falter as we seek to follow your way; our gaze is turned away from awareness of your glory to preoccupation with our own needs and concerns; and even our love for one another grows cold. We trust only in your grace to create new life within us and to bind us together in love and common commitment. Let your spirit be born in us anew, and accept our lives, which we offer to you. Amen.

The Act of Covenant

LITURGIST: Choose this day whom you will serve, and whom you will worship. Will you worship and serve Yahweh in sincerity and faithfulness, or will you follow after other gods?[1]

PEOPLE: Far be it from us that we should forsake Yahweh to serve other gods, for it is Yahweh our God who has brought us and our ancestors up from the land of Egypt, out of the house of bondage, and who has done great things in our sight.[2]

LITURGIST: And what are the deeds to which you testify?

At this point the congregation will say the United Church of Christ Statement of Faith or another appropriate creed.

LITURGIST: Do you commit yourselves today to take up the cost and joy of discipleship to Jesus Christ during the coming year and henceforth?

PEOPLE: As we begin this new year, we renew our covenant with one another to seek and respond to the word and the will of God. We purpose to walk together in all God's ways, made known and yet to be made known to us. We will join in the mission of the church to witness to the gospel of Jesus Christ in all the world, while worshiping God and striving for truth, justice, and peace, relying on the Holy Spirit to lead and empower us. We will pray for the coming of the realm of God, and we look with faith toward the triumph of righteousness and eternal life. This we will do, with the help of God.

Words of Institution

PASTOR: We have confessed our inadequacy before Almighty God. We have professed our reliance on the grace of God. We have renewed our commitment to follow Jesus Christ, and to participate in God's mission in the world. I invite you now to share in the bread and the wine of the new covenant in Jesus Christ. *(The pastor will now say the Words of Institution.)*

Distribution of the Elements
Prayer of Thanksgiving

ALL: Faithful God, we are thankful that you have revealed to us the vision of life in covenant with you and with one another. We are thankful that you have sent Jesus Christ to invite people of all ages, tongues, and races into faithful covenant, and that Christ is present with us in the breaking of bread. Through your Spirit, strengthen us to be faithful in all we have promised today. Amen.

(RCD)

NOTE: This service is based on Joshua 24, the United Church of Christ liturgy and Statement of Faith, and the Constitution of Bethel-Bethany UCC. Each congregation might change the prayer before the Words of Institution to reflect its own constitution. This service was inspired by a Covenant Renewal Service at the Parish of the Holy Covenant (United Methodist) Chicago.

An Order of Worship for Communion* (Based on Early Christian Worship and the Book of Revelation)

Call to Worship[3]

LEADER: Grace unto you and peace from God, who was and who is, and who is to come,

PEOPLE: And from Jesus Christ, the faithful witness, the first born of the dead, ruler above all rulers of the earth.

LEADER: In love Jesus Christ suffered death to free us from our sins,

PEOPLE: Making us a nation of priests set aside for God's service.

ALL: To Jesus Christ be the glory and power forever and ever! Amen.

Old Testament Reading: Exodus 15:1-18
Renewal of Baptismal Vows

The Marks of the Beast and of the Lamb: A reading from Revelation 13:11-12, 16-17, 14:1-5.†

Questions for Reflection

1. What are the signs of the beast (oppression, cruelty, sin) in our world today? Are there ways in which I am marked by them?
2. How am I marked as a faithful witness to Jesus Christ?
3. What is the meaning of baptism in the world today? What is the meaning of my baptism?
4. What is one way in which I would like to become more faithful to Jesus Christ?

The Kiss of Peace

LEADER: The time for reflection will be followed by a quiet time of sharing with one or two persons. When you are through, "mark" one another on the forehead with the sign of Christ (a cross or a fish), saying, "The grace and peace of Christ be yours." The response is: "And yours."

---

* This service is especially appropriate for the Easter season, because it emphasizes the resurrection appearances when Jesus ate with his disciples.

† Part of the early Christian rite of baptism was a symbolic marking of the forehead with the sign of Christ. People also wore white robes for baptism, a symbol that appears often in the book of Revelation. To be baptized was a risky thing for some early Christians.

Prayer of Confession

ALL: O living Christ, as we gather at your table we are aware that sometimes our love toward God grows cold, and our willingness to serve grows lukewarm.[4] Forgive us, and grant that all those who have been sealed by your name in baptism may faithfully keep their vows, and thus receive the crown of life.[5] Amen.

LEADER: In baptism we have been marked with the life of Christ, and set free from sin and death. To Christ be praise and glory!

PEOPLE: Alleluia! Amen.

At this point the Gospel may be read and the Sermon preached.

The Prayers of the Faithful

Reading

Revelation 8:1-5 *(to be accompanied by the burning of incense)*

Silence

Prayers *(beginning on page 17, The Hymnal of the United Church of Christ; or other bidding-type prayers)*

Act of Communion with Jesus Christ and One Another

Offering of Bread and Wine and Other Gifts

Doxology

Eucharistic Litany

LEADER: God be with you.

PEOPLE: And with your spirit.

LEADER: Lift up your hearts.

PEOPLE: We lift them up to God.

LEADER: Let us give thanks to God, Creator, Christ, and Holy Spirit.

PEOPLE: Great and wonderful are your deeds, O God Almighty. Just and true are your ways, O Ruler of the ages.[6] We give you thanks, for you have created all things, and by your will they exist.[7] You have delivered your people from bondage, and you have given to us Jesus Christ, Lamb of God, Savior of the world, who has won for us the victory over sin and death and all evil.

ALL: Holy, holy, holy,
God of love and majesty,
The whole universe speaks of your majesty,
O God, Most High.[8]

LEADER: Glory be to you, O Christ, for you were slain, and by your blood you ransomed for God people from every tribe, tongue, people and nation. You have made them a nation of priests to serve our God, and they shall reign on earth.[9]

PEOPLE: The Lamb who was slain is worthy to receive power and wealth, wisdom and might, honor, glory, and blessing.[10]

ALL: Spirit of God, touch our lives deeply, and make us truly yours; and bless these gifts of bread and wine. O living Christ, bright morning star[11] of this darkened world, come and be our guest. Name us, mark us, and claim us as your own. Free us from bondage to the powers of this world. Glory be to you! Amen.

Invitation *(Could be based on Revelation 3:20)*

Words of Institution and the Distribution of the Elements

Prayer of Thanksgiving

ALL: God Almighty, who is and who was, we give you thanks that you have taken your great power and have begun to reign![12] We thank you for this feast of love and victory, which is a foretaste of the day when all the faithful shall gather, reunited with Christ the Lamb. May that day come soon! Give us courage to serve you in costly obedience, that your ways of justice and truth may triumph on this earth. Amen.

A hymn may be sung and the Benediction given. Place other hymns as appropriate for your congregation.

(RCD)

NOTE: This service is based on and paraphrases parts of the book of Revelation and was inspired by Oscar Cullmann, *Early Christian Worship, Studies in Biblical Theology* (Naperville, IL: Alec R. Allenson, 1953); Massey H. Shepherd, Jr., *The Paschal Liturgy and the Apocalypse* (Richmond: John Knox Press, 1960); and Catherine G. González and Justo Luis González, *Vision at Patmos,* 1978 (United Methodist Service Center, 7820 Reading Road, Cincinnati, OH 45237).

A Liturgy for Worldwide Communion Sunday

The Invitation

Come, people of God, out of your separateness, to enter into unity with one another, and with all those who seek the presence of Jesus Christ, through the breaking of bread and the sharing of wine. Come, confessing the sin that separates you from God and from one another.

Prayer of Confession

Eternal God of all people and places, we confess to you our lack of oneness with our human sisters and brothers as we begin this celebration of unity in Christ. We have closed our ears to voices of pain, and of wisdom, when they speak in accents other than our own. We have lacked the vision to see that people living in places we call foreign are as surely your children as we are. Our sensibilities are jarred even by the way our nearest neighbors express their faith in Christ. We cling to the pride of nation and denomination as if we had a special claim on truth and leadership.

Gracious God, forgive us, and renew a right spirit within us, a spirit of compassion, understanding, and humility. Fill us with the vision of unity in Christ, and enable us to incarnate Christ's love, so that we may worthily partake in the body of Christ and the wine of the new covenant. Amen.

Words of Assurance and Praise

The good news in Christ is that God is more willing to forgive our sins than we are to acknowledge them. The God of peace be with you all, keeping you in unity with Christ's people everywhere, with whom we sing this ancient song of praise.

LEADER: We praise you, O God.

PEOPLE: We acknowledge you as the rightful object of our worship and obedience.

LEADER: All earth worships you.

PEOPLE: Heaven and earth are full of the majesty of your glory.

LEADER: The glorious company of the apostles praise you.

PEOPLE: The goodly communion of the prophets praise you.

ALL: Day by day we glorify you, and we worship your name forever, world without end. Amen. [13]

Prayer of Consecration

We give you thanks, O God, for the mighty sweep of your love, embracing all people and all nations. We thank you that you have sent Jesus Christ to us to break down the walls of hostility which divide the earth's people, and to reveal your all-encompassing love, making us all one. Through the power of your Spirit, may this unity become reality.

Now, by your presence, make sacred this feast in memory of Jesus Christ. As this broken bread was scattered like grain on the hillsides, and then, when gathered together, became one loaf, so may your church be gathered together from the ends of the earth into your eternal realm. [14] Like Christ, who was offered up to you that we might live, and like this wine, which was poured out that all might share in the signs of new life, so may the lives of your people be poured out in compassion, and in solidarity with the poor, the oppressed, and the hungry of this world. For it is in the name of Jesus Christ, your Servant, that we pray. Amen.

Words of Institution

Distribution of the Elements

Prayer of Thanksgiving

God of new life, with joy we have received this sacrament of bread and wine, giving you thanks for Jesus Christ, our peace and our hope. Unite your church throughout the world in continuing Christ's ministry of love and servanthood, that your name may be praised in all the earth. Amen.

(RCD)

An Order for Confirmation

Declaration of Faith *(minister and confirmands)*

Do you believe in God the creator of the universe, who calls us each into relationship with God and with one another?

RESPONSE: We do.

Do you believe in Jesus Christ as the revealing expression of God's love come to dwell among the human family?

RESPONSE: We do.

Do you believe in the Holy Spirit as the force by which we are brought into closer harmony with the will of God?

RESPONSE: We do.

Do you then as persons who have declared your faith before this gathered company seek to become one in spirit with the membership of _____ Church?

In so doing, do you pledge to enter into an honest and open relationship of mutual support and nurture with this congregation?

Do you pledge to maintain this body through your personal efforts and talents?

Do you pledge to further the work of God's realm and the church universal by studied and prayerful efforts to serve all humanity after the manner of Jesus Christ?

Finally, do you pledge to challenge the limits of your faith through education, prayer, reflection, and examination?

RESPONSE: We do.

Sharing of the Covenant

CONFIRMANDS: I promise to take Jesus Christ as the Authority of my life. I promise that, with God's help, I will earnestly strive to live as Christ would have me live. I accept my responsibilities as a member of this church and promise to support it in all its mission to the best of my ability.

MINISTER AND CONGREGATION: Do you as members of _____ Church receive with open spirits these persons into communion here? Are you willing to accept their needs for support and guidance? Are you willing to accept also the challenge and questions they bring with them? Finally, are you willing at all times to cherish and preserve herein a sense of Christian love and engage yourselves with these new members in harmonious community, seeking always God's will?

RESPONSE: We do.

(DK)

A Litany for Reception of New Members

LITURGIST: The church is a family of people with varieties of gifts, united by the Spirit revealed in Jesus of Nazareth.

PEOPLE: It is the Spirit of caring for one another, of forgiving, of helping each other, of love revealed in the life and death of Jesus.

NEW MEMBERS: We want to share in that Spirit!

LITURGIST: The church is the people of God, with a diversity of needs, ideas, and visions, inspired by the Spirit burning through the words and deeds of Jesus as recorded in scripture. (Read Luke 4:14-21.) May that same Spirit rest upon us.

PEOPLE: It is the Spirit of openness to the world and to all people as our sisters and brothers, of continual searching and learning and of saying, "We believe, help our unbelief."[15] It is the stirring toward growth and renewal that takes many forms.

NEW MEMBERS: We want to share in that Spirit!

LITURGIST: The Spirit of the Christ calls us into a life of servanthood unto suffering.

PEOPLE: The Suffering Servant is one who is despised and rejected, a person of sorrows and well acquainted with grief.[16] The Suffering Servant bears the grief and sorrows of others, and through suffering brings wholeness.

NEW MEMBERS: We want to share in that Spirit!

LITURGIST: The Spirit of the Christ which was present with Jesus is the Spirit of the Exodus—the Spirit that opts for liberation.

PEOPLE: The cries of the brick-makers in Egypt and throughout history have been heard by the God of the Exodus.

NEW MEMBERS: We want to share in that Spirit!

LITURGIST: The Spirit of the Christ which was present with Jesus is the Spirit of covenant formation, of community-building.

PEOPLE:	We stand at the end of a cloud of witnesses [17] that include Abraham and Sarah, Miriam and Moses, Esther and David, Job's daughters and the sons of the prophets, Martha and Jesus, and brothers and sisters in our midst who stand open to the Spirit's bidding.
NEW MEMBERS:	We want to share in that Spirit!
LITURGIST:	The Spirit of the Christ is also the Ruler of creation.
PEOPLE:	The Spirit that was the creative brooding Presence in the midst of the waters of chaos is still moving in our midst and in the midst of the ongoing creation of the world to bring order out of chaos, unity in the midst of disunity, life in the midst of death.
NEW MEMBERS:	We want to share in that Spirit!
LITURGIST:	I present these persons to this community of faith in the hope that the Spirit of Christ might rest upon each of us and all of us together. May the Spirit of the resurrected Christ make us into that Body which is of Christ.

(WUMC)

A Funeral Service*

Prelude

Call to Awareness

LEADER:	We have gathered to celebrate the life of _____.
PEOPLE:	We give thanks for (his/her) life; we receive (his/her) death as a gift; we commend (his/her) spirit into God's eternal being.
LEADER:	Let us recall all the saints who have found that Peace, that Shalom, in which _____ now rests. Let us sing of their faith.

Hymn: "For All the Saints"

Recalling the Life

Psalm 102
The story of _____'s life.

Song: "It's a Long Road to Freedom"

Sharing from the Community—Songs of Faith

Gathering for Offering and Prayer

Hearing the Word

---

* This service was prepared to celebrate the life of Dewey Olson, a member of Wheadon United Methodist Church.

Scripture: 2 Corinthians 5:7
Sermon: "We Walk by Faith, Not Sight"

Song of Faith: "Glory Be to God on High"

Greeting One Another in Christ's Name

The Sending Forth

LEADER: Christ went before us in death, as has our loved one, showing us the way into eternal life.

PEOPLE: We celebrate the good life we have shared with _____.

LEADER: God has given. God has received that which was loaned to us.

PEOPLE: We are thankful for the good days we shared.

LEADER: May God our Creator and Jesus our Christ fortify in us every good deed and word.

PEOPLE: The grace of Jesus Christ, the love of God, and the communion of the Holy Spirit be with us all.

LEADER: Amen.

PEOPLE: Amen!

(WUMC)

Time-Markers:
Resources for the Church Year

Reflections on the Church Year

In several of the communities out of which these materials grew, worship is shaped very much by the turning of the church year. This rhythm of reflection can bring together themes from the biblical story, especially God's revelation in Jesus Christ with the basic human issues of life stories today.

Advent, celebrated the four Sundays before Christmas, recalls times of waiting and expectancy, and expresses our present yearnings for that which is not yet born within us. Christmastide is a time of wonder at the Word becoming flesh, of God's coming to share our common lot in Jesus Christ, calling forth wonder at the sacred in the midst of flesh-and-blood existence. The season passes in two short weeks, and we enter Epiphany, a season of many meanings lasting eight or nine weeks. Epiphany is the time of God's presence being revealed in the midst of human life—in the ministry of Jesus Christ, but also in the church, and indeed everywhere. The coming of the magi is remembered as a sign of God's care for all people; thus Epiphany is also a time of special focus on global concerns.

Lent, the forty days before Easter, is a time of awareness of limits—the limits of human sin, frailty, and death—as we remember how Jesus Christ and the Exodus people struggled with these realities in themselves and in the world around them. The seven Sundays of Eastertide are a joyous season, when we proclaim that God breaks through all these human limits, bringing wholeness and new life. The season of Pentecost explores life in an age when God's reign has not yet been fully established on earth, but when the Holy Spirit is given to all who seek, to enable them to participate in God's reign when it breaks through in their time and place.

Although resources for only one year are included here, many of them were created with passages from the lectionary in mind. For example, Call to Worship number 3 for Advent is based on the Old Testament reading for the Third Sunday in Advent, Series A. Where possible, scripture-based materials are close to lectionary order. However, if your congregation does not follow the church year or lectionary closely, you may find the resources under "Pentecost (and General)" most helpful.

Advent

Calls to Worship

1. LEADER: Now is the time of watching and waiting.

PEOPLE: The time of pregnant expectation of new life.

LEADER: Now is the season of hope unfolding.

PEOPLE: The dark winter season when hope is waiting to be born.

LEADER: Let us come before God with receptive and willing spirits.

PEOPLE: May our souls magnify God's name and may our spirits rejoice in God our Savior![1]

ALL: Rejoice! God comes to bring the birthday of life and hope. Amen.

(RCD)

2. LEADER: Let the heavens be glad, let the earth rejoice before the God of all peoples,

PEOPLE: For God comes in power to judge the earth.

LEADER: Let us open our hearts in worship and trust, and offer our lives in willing service,

PEOPLE: For God shall judge the world with righteousness, and the peoples with truth.[2]

(PJF)

3. LEADER: The wilderness shall be glad, and the desert shall blossom.

PEOPLE: All flesh will see God's majesty and glory.

LEADER: You with weak hands, God will strengthen you!

PEOPLE: You who are fearful, take heart!

LEADER: For behold, God is coming to save the faithful.

PEOPLE: They will obtain joy and gladness, and sorrow and sighing shall flee away.

ALL: Let us rejoice and sing, for our God comes! Amen.[3]

(RCD)

4. LEADER: Behold! God is good, and has set a star in the heavens to guide us to the truth.

PEOPLE: We follow it with joy, knowing that God will give us strength to climb the hills, and sight to conquer the darkness.

LEADER: Behold! God is good, and has promised us a Savior to lead us to righteousness.

PEOPLE: We await the Savior's coming with gladness and with expectation that in the holy birth our lives may be renewed.

(PJF)

5. *(For a Communion Sunday in Advent)*

LEADER : Like the Israelites, who praised you in the midst of preparations to leave Egypt,

PEOPLE : Like Jesus and the disciples, who celebrated their oneness with you in the midst of crisis,

LEADER : We turn to you, O God, in the midst of our lives.

PEOPLE : We gather at your table to remember your mighty works of old.

LEADER : We lay our hopes and fears before you, in joyful anticipation of the future you are bringing into being.

ALL : Thanks be to you, O God, for your presence with us now and always. Amen.

(RCD)

6. *(For Christmas Eve)*

LEADER : Come away, come away, come today to Bethlehem.

PEOPLE : Come adore on bended knee, one whose birth the angels sing.

LEADER : Come away, come away, from your noisy celebration, to a place of quietness and peace.

PEOPLE : Come with wonder, come with awe. Take your place among sheep and cattle.

ALL : Sing with joy, praise God, for the time of promise has come. Sing the good news of Emmanuel: God-with-us! The Christ has come!

LEADER : Come away, come away, come today to Bethlehem.

The congregation then sings "O Little Town of Bethlehem"

(RCD)

Prayers of Confession

1. God of the Past, in the wilderness of Jordan you sent a messenger to prepare human hearts for the coming of the Christ. We rejoice that through the centuries that message of hope has brought confidence and joy to people.

God of the Present, even now you are among us. Forgive us that often we have failed to discern your presence with us, and have felt deserted and alone. Make strong in our hearts the faith that enables us to live serenely and triumphantly.

God of the Future, you have promised that Christ's reign is coming. Teach us to live in expectation, that what we are and do today may be anchored in the certainty of your tomorrow. Through the grace of Jesus Christ. Amen.

(PJF)

2. As followers of Christ, we are always on a journey. On our pilgrimage there is no time when we can afford to stop growing in love, in strength, and in knowledge of God. So it is that when we gather to worship we must confess those places in which we need to grow. In preparation for the coming of the Christ, let us confess our need for growth, in silence before God: *(Silent prayer of confession)*

Words of Assurance

The good news in Christ is that when we face ourselves and God with the awareness of our need, we are given grace to grow, and courage to continue the journey. Amen.

(RCD)

3. God of steadfast love, how impatient we are with you, with each other, and with ourselves! We do not live as those who recognize your reign on earth, though we are again celebrating its arrival. Our children, parents, and friends receive our anger too often and our expressions of love and interest too rarely. We expend our compassion in dinner-table conversations about the evening news, and satisfy our desire for justice by reading the morning editorial page. We try to absolve our responsibility to relatives and friends through the annual ritual of gifts and cards. We speak of love and peace on earth, but ignore the realities and needs of our brothers and sisters in the global community. We earnestly repent, and are sorry in our hearts for these shortcomings and misdoings. We ask your forgiveness. Please give us the vision, strength, and will to *expect* and *live* in your dynamic, caring, and brooding presence—Now! Amen.

(WUMC)

4. Almighty God, Light of the World, you caused light to shine out of darkness in the advent of Jesus our Christ; you continually open to us the ways we are to prepare. We confess our unwillingness to see the light and to walk in your ways. We have not always opened our eyes to the needs of others, and our feet have wandered from the paths of justice and peace. We ask that the Spirit of Christ be born anew within us, that our hearts may be stirred to glorify the nativity with acts of compassion and service. Amen.

(MAN)

5. *(For Christmas Eve)* O Holy One, who surrounds our lives with grace, we confess that our eyes are dull. Your presence in our lives takes us by surprise. We see only the outer signs: the baby, the feeding-place for cattle, the tired mother and father. Help us to know you, not only in the angels' song, but in the ordinary happenings of our lives, that we may be channels of your grace in Jesus Christ. Amen.

(RCD)

Collective Prayers

1. O Living Christ, you were, you are, you come. Clothe us with garments of celebration, that we may be prepared for the feast of your reign. Keep us wakeful, that our lamps may ever burn in the vigil of your coming. Give us sight, that we may recognize the signs of your coming. And give us the strength to stand in your presence. So may all these things be, through your gracious Spirit. Amen.

(RCD)

2. Eternal Source of hope and of human destiny, we await impatiently your fuller revelation in time and history. Through the coming of Christ, and through the commitment of our lives, reign among us on earth. Amen.

(RCD)

3. God of the wilderness, God of the wastelands of our lives, lead us apart to those places where we hear your word most clearly. In the startling awareness of Christ's coming, may we order our lives with repentance and with compassion. Sift from our lives all useless chaff, that like good wheat into a barn, we may be gathered into the realm of your righteousness, through the grace of Jesus Christ. Amen.

(RCD)

4. O living Christ, we need your love today to shine in the dark corners of our world, where loneliness and hatred, war and suffering, greed and lust destroy. Come to us and shine in our lives, that we may more perfectly love you and reflect your love on earth. Amen.

(RCD)

5. *(For Christmas Eve)* We praise you, hidden God, that in Jesus Christ you have come to us to speak your Word of love and life. Touch us with unearthly joy, like the singing of angels; fill us with wonder, like the eyes of children; teach us to humble ourselves before you, like the worshiping magi. May our journey to the manger be only the beginning of a lifetime of service to Jesus our Christ. Amen.

(RCD)

Christmastide

Calls to Worship

1. *(Christmas Day)*
Sing "O Come, All Ye Faithful" before or after

LEADER: Come, all that are faithful, and all that seek faith.

PEOPLE: It is the season to sing and rejoice!

LEADER: The symbol of new hope and spirit shines, the spirit of peace.

PEOPLE: And we would follow and find that peace.

LEADER: We now have a promise fulfilled by God,

PEOPLE: That the Christ who is born will call us to a new life of faith and action! Amen.

(KF)

2. LEADER: Christ is born!

PEOPLE: Christ *is* born!

LEADER: Because of this birth, life is full of promise for you and for me. Life is full of promise for our community.

PEOPLE: We celebrate today the presence of God's promise in our midst.

LEADER: The promise of a small child coming into a crowded, hurting world, and growing to be a liberator.

PEOPLE: It's the promise of you and me, struggling and stumbling together, growing and celebrating, reaching out to make a new presence in our world.

(WUMC)

3. LEADER: Let us sing praise to the God of all creation.

PEOPLE: Let us sing praise to the Spirit who gives life to all.

LEADER: Let us sing praise to Jesus Christ, in whom the fullness of God was pleased to dwell,

PEOPLE: That everything and everyone in all creation might be reunited with God through Christ.

ALL: We sing with the faithful of all ages, tongues, and races![4]

(RCD)

Prayers of Confession

1. Faithful God, we rejoice that you have sent your promised Christ. And yet, O God, we confess that we are still not ready for Christ's coming; we are reluctant to live as if the whole earth were your domain. We know the story—the shepherds, the angels, the magi—but we don't fully understand what it means. Awaken us to your Spirit, let Christ's birth make a difference in our lives, and grant us your peace, through the grace of Jesus Christ. Amen.

(RCD)

2. O God, the Baby has come, and we see that we are waiting for ourselves. We delay changing our lives, in the small ways as well as the large. It is hard to work for systemic change from within the system, and still harder to remain objective in the midst of our struggle. For these and other failings, we are most sorry. We pray for strength and wisdom, that we may better carry out your word this coming week. *(Silent meditation)*

LEADER: Lift up your hearts.

PEOPLE: We lift them up to God.

LEADER: Let us give thanks to God, for those who repent are forgiven and strengthened in goodness.

ALL: Amen.

(WUMC)

3. *(For the new year)* Eternal God, who can make all things new, we humbly bring before you the record of our lives in the year now ending. Where life has been good to us, do not let us take more of the credit than we deserve. Where we have been good to others, help us to forget all thoughts of honor and reward. Where we have fallen short, forgive us, and free us from brooding over what is past. Cleanse us by your mercy, guide us by your truth, fill us with your love, lead us forward in your all-conquering hope. Through the grace of Jesus Christ. Amen.

(PJF)

Collective Prayers

1. *(Christmas Day)* Out of the noise and glitter and ho-ho-ho of the world's Christmas, we have come away, O God, into this hour in your presence. Help us to discover here the true meaning and joy that lie beneath the surface of the holy day. Help us to see beyond the Baby in the manger to the man Jesus became, to test our lives by teachings and example. Enable us to see beyond the human Jesus to your own incredible love reaching out to us through him, giving wisdom and power for the journeys of our lives. Then send us out to spread the word that you are born among us. Through Jesus Christ we pray. Amen.

(PJF)

2. Living God, moved by the coming of Christ to our lives, we seek to be your people. Help us to live in faithful covenant with you and with one another. Let the peace of Christ guide us, and let Christ's message in all its richness live in our hearts, that we may praise you without ceasing. Amen.[5]

(RCD)

3. Amazing God, you have confounded the wisdom of this world by coming to us in the form of a human baby, frail and vulnerable. Help us to comprehend the great love

with which you open yourself to our world, that we in turn may risk to open ourselves in love toward all your children, and that we may find the source of our lives in Jesus Christ and the folly of the cross. Amen.[6]

(RCD)

Additional Resources for Christmastide

A Litany of Confession

LEADER: Before our sisters and brothers here, we each can admit that we have failed to live trusting God.

VOICE 1: The world at our doorstep throws itself at us in so many thousands of ways. It is hard to see promise in making any kind of response.

ALL: We hear so much about revolution and liberation that has to do with confrontation and violence; it scares us! Where's the promise in that?

VOICE 2: It is not an easy thing to see promise in the day-to-day mundane chores that have to be done.

ALL: We are busy running a church, maintaining a home, working at a job. Where's the promise in that?

VOICE 3: The word comes to us that somehow our Creator understands what it is like to be human, but it is hard to relate to an Advent so far in the past.

ALL: We know inside ourselves that we face life and death alone. It is tempting to see the promise as only a promise of death.

VOICE 4: Is the Christ really that sister, that brother, sitting with me, working with me, challenging me, bugging me, loving me?

ALL: Another kid comes into the world! Helpless, and demanding so much from us. Another revolutionary is crushed because we have too much stake in the status quo. Where's the promise in that? When we have been unable to see the promise, we have acted cynically, selfishly, carelessly. We confess the need for a new beginning, an advent, in our lives and in our world. Amen.

LEADER: We know that Exodus does not stop in wandering, and that Advent does not end on a cross. Within and through persons, our Creator renews and fulfills the promise of new life. That doesn't stop being true just because we can't see it, feel it, or act on it. It comes as each sister and brother responds to our confession with forgiveness. Turn to someone near you and offer the words "I forgive you."

(WUMC)

Song of Anna (LAUS DEO)

I praise you, O God,

25

For I have seen the Redeemer of Israel,
the Liberator of Jerusalem!
Many years have I been fasting and praying,
But now I will leave the temple and proclaim the Word for all.
For it is written,
"Rejoice, rejoice, daughter of Zion,
shout aloud, daughter of Jerusalem,
Lo, your ruler comes to you
Speaking peaceably to every nation,
And the reign shall extend from sea to sea
From the river to the ends of the earth."

Glory to the Creator, and to Christ, and to the Holy Spirit, as it was in the beginning, is now, and will be forever. Amen.[7]

(MJS)

Pastoral Benediction

The Word has become flesh and dwelt among us.[8] Let Christ's light shine in the darkest corner of your life. Let Christ's love shine in the darkest corners of our world. God is with us. Alleluia. Amen.

(RCD)

Epiphany

Calls to Worship

1. LEADER: We have come to praise God, who has done wonderful things among us.

   PEOPLE: In Jesus, the Christ, God has shown us love, giving light for our darkness, and strength for all our days.

   LEADER: Sing praise to God's name, bow before God in prayer, open your hearts to God's saving word.

   PEOPLE: Arise, shine, for your light has come!

(PJF)

2. LEADER: We are here to praise God because Jesus Christ has set us free to live.

   PEOPLE: We are here because in Christ we are forgiven and made whole.

   LEADER: We are gathered because Jesus Christ has united us into one family of faith.

   ALL: We will witness to the good news: Jesus Christ frees and unites. Praise God! Alleluia! Amen.

(RCD)

3. LEADER: From the midst of our real lives with their very real problems,

   PEOPLE: We come to seek courage and strength from the presence of God and the support of one another.

   LEADER: As persons who love imperfectly and are loved imperfectly,

   PEOPLE: We come to be renewed by the perfect love of God, proclaimed in the community of love and faith.

   LEADER: As persons who never fully live up to their high calling in Jesus Christ,

   PEOPLE: We come to be encouraged to do our best for one more week.

   ALL: Let us worship, with hearts open to the love of God, with hands outstretched to one another, and with whole selves willing to accept the cost and joy of being Christ's disciples. Amen.

(RCD)

4. LEADER: Welcome, travelers.

   PEOPLE: Welcome.

   LEADER: Sometimes it is harder to cross an unrepaired sidewalk than travel a thousand miles.

   PEOPLE: Sometimes it is harder to forgive an old friend than to welcome a stranger.

   LEADER: But God teaches us that we should welcome the stranger as we would welcome Jesus Christ.

   ALL: However far we have come this week, we bring gifts of our selves, our minds, our compassion, our love, and our dedication. Let us continue our journey together.

(WUMC)

5. LEADER: This is God's world! To us is given a vision of nations and races, lands and people, joined together in love.

   PEOPLE: Praise be to God, the Creator, in whose image we are created.

   LEADER: We come to celebrate and renew that vision, opening ourselves to the One who is its source and its living fire.

   PEOPLE: We affirm in Christ that we can be, and are, one world and one family, working together to manifest God's rule in the lives of all people![9]

(CB)

6. LEADER: Awake, my soul!

   PEOPLE: Awake, O harp and trumpet!

   LEADER: We will give thanks to you, O God, among the peoples.

PEOPLE:	We will sing praises to you among the nations.
LEADER:	For your compassion is greater than the heavens.
PEOPLE:	Your faithfulness reaches to the clouds.
ALL:	Be exalted, O God, above the heavens! Let your glory cover the earth![10]

(RCD)

7. LEADER: Come, gather together like those who sat at Jesus' feet so many years ago.

PEOPLE: We gather with joy, for we too want to be disciples of Christ.

LEADER: I tell you, Christ is here with us, calling us now to life and love.

PEOPLE: Let us praise God for bringing us together, and coming to us in Jesus Christ. Amen.

(RCD)

8. LEADER: This is what God has spoken: "Keep justice and righteousness,

PEOPLE: For soon my salvation will come, and my deliverance will be revealed.

LEADER: All who hold fast my covenant, these I will bring to my holy mountain,

PEOPLE: And make them joyful in my house of prayer.

LEADER: Their burnt offerings and their sacrifices will be accepted on my altar,

PEOPLE: For my house shall be called a house of prayer for all peoples!"[11]

(MSG)

9. LEADER: Welcome to our worship.

PEOPLE: Greetings to our brothers and sisters in the faith.

LEADER: We come to celebrate God's presence.

PEOPLE: And God's love expressed through Jesus Christ.

LEADER: We come remembering Christ's life and ministry.

PEOPLE: And the life we are called to live.

LEADER: We come as a pilgrim people searching for ways to live out our faith.

PEOPLE: We come seeking the strength to carry on our journey.

ALL: Let us rejoice in God's gift to us!

(WUMC)

Prayers of Confession

1. Almighty God, as the church, we are part of your redeeming work in history. Yet we know that often we seek our own success and salvation, and fear to follow Christ in commitment to a vision of wholeness for the world and its peoples. Help us to speak

and act our parts in the great drama of your love, and in the freeing gospel of Jesus Christ, in whose name we pray. Amen.

Words of Assurance

PASTOR: Hear the good news! God has forgiven each one of us and calls us to take our parts in the drama of redeeming love.

PEOPLE: Praise God, who accepts and uses our very human lives in the unfolding story of salvation and new life!

(RCD)

2. Let us confess together that we have not always lived as those forgiven, set free, and united in Christ: O God, Source of life and grace, we are aware that we are, at times, prisoners of fear and habit. Through the healing touch of Christ, set us free to live and to love, that we may be the people you have created us to be. Amen.

Words of Assurance

The good news is that Christ calls us to new life and enables us to begin again and again and again. Let us praise God with songs of joy!

(RCD)

3. O God, Spirit of Power, we confess that at times we come to you seeking miracles, but only for ourselves. We confess that we withhold the gifts you bestow on us for service, using them only for our own benefit. Open our eyes, that we may trust your wonder-working power and allow that power to work in us, and through us for others. We pray in the mighty name of Jesus Christ. Amen.

(RCD)

4. God of all creation, Ruler of all peoples, you know us completely, how mean we are and how good we are. We humbly confess the mistakes we have made and the good we have neglected, the promises we have broken and the duties we have refused. Let the power and joy of your love become a mighty force in our lives. Help us to develop the good that is in us, and not be afraid to use it. Fortify our decision to live with honesty, integrity, joy, and unselfishness, through the grace of Jesus Christ. Amen.

(PJF)

5. Holy One, before your splendor and glory we fall silent, aware of our human frailty and sin. Who are we to speak your word of love, or spread your gospel of truth? Yet only speak your word of forgiveness, only touch us with your healing fire, and humbly we will respond to your call, through the grace of Jesus Christ. Amen.

(RCD)

6. Eternal God, we confess that we do not expect and long for the transforming power of your love to work miracles in these hard hearts of ours. Yet we secretly long for a

rescue, an escape, a miracle, to relieve us of the responsibilities and the challenges you set before us. Healing Spirit, renew our confidence in your power and in the power of love to change our lives, and give us courage to be the fully responsible persons Christ calls us to be. Amen.

(RCD)

7. ALL: You have called us, God, to live as Christ did. It is difficult. We confess to you and to ourselves how often we fall short of Christ's example.

LEADER: We have gone off after our own goals, forgetting to test them by your intention for us. *(Pause)* We have failed to understand the needs of those around us and seek their good. *(Pause)* We have relied on our own strength and given in to despair, when we ought to have turned to you. *(Pause)*

ALL: Cleanse and renew us, that we may know the joy of your presence and be bearers of your light, through the grace of Jesus Christ. Amen.

(PJF)

8. Gracious God, Creator and Redeemer, in reverence we bow before you, giving thanks for your love and seeking your grace. Humbly we acknowledge that you have blessed us and called us to be your servants in the world. Yet we confess that we have hoarded more than our share of the world's bounty; that in silence we have consented to the oppression of our sisters and brothers; that we have failed to witness, by word and action, to the liberating truth of Jesus Christ. In Christ's name, forgive us and grant us a new birth of spirit, that we may be your instruments of oneness and of joy, of healing and of peace. Amen.

(PJF)

9. O Source of all true wisdom and goodness, how often we substitute our own wisdom and goodness for the way of life shown to us by Jesus Christ. Forgive us, open our hearts to the simple, gentle, loving ways Jesus taught, and empower us by your Spirit so to live. Amen.

(RCD)

Collective Prayers

1. O God, our Maker, whose eye regards even the sparrow, you care for this world you have made, with tenderness. Through your loving Spirit, you seek to redeem your lost creation and to make it whole again. So it was, you sent your Christ, as a servant, to bind up our brokenness and heal our wounded spirits. Grant that we might be receptive to Christ's healing touch, that we may be made whole and set free to love. Amen.

(RCD)

2. Redeemer God, we thank you for the newness of life you offer us in Jesus Christ. Through your Spirit, cast out our fear and all our diseases. Make us free indeed. Amen.

(RCD)

3. God of the faithful in every time, today you have called us into your church to be one body in Jesus Christ. You have bestowed upon us the gifts we need for your service. Grant that we may willingly take our part; that we may support one another; and that we may seek the greatest gift, which is love. Knead us together into one loaf with all your people throughout the world, through your Spirit of unity. Amen.

(RCD)

4. Living Christ, your earthly ministry was full of struggle as well as joy; yet you were faithful in following God's will. Breathe your Spirit into our lives, that we may never fall back from the way of discipleship or the effort of loving. Grant that we may find true joy and peace as we accept the cost of faithful discipleship. For it is in your name we pray. Amen.

(RCD)

5. O God, we are awed by the responsibility you entrust to us as your children, that you ask us to point the way toward you. Help us to be like salt, a small ingredient that gives flavor to the common life of humanity while drawing little attention to itself. Give us courage to live with faith, love, and hope through Christ, so that our lives may shine with your light, and all may worship you. Amen.

(RCD)

6. God of all joy, we give you thanks that in the epiphany of Jesus Christ you have shown us the way to true life. We praise you that you receive as your children those who seek peace and righteousness, and that you make your promise of eternal life to the humble, the merciful, and the pure in heart. Enable us, like Christ, to find our happiness in doing your will, so that we too may live to love and serve you forever. Amen.[12]

(RCD)

7. God of grace and glory, we thank you that you judge us not by the perfection of our actions, but by our readiness to live boldly by faith. Help us, as individuals and as a congregation, to trust you and follow where you lead, that in Christ your name may be glorified in all the earth. Amen.

(RCD)

8. O Spirit that flows through all life, you were powerfully present in the life and ministry of Jesus. Yet many of his contemporaries were looking for something more dramatic, someone less simple. Like them, we do not always recognize your presence. Give us spirits that respond to your Spirit as an instrument resounds to a musician's touch, that we may glorify your name in Christ Jesus. Amen.

(RCD)

9. God of infinite love, who through Jesus Christ shared our life, and communed with tax collectors and sinners, we rejoice that you come to us and seek us where we are and as we are. We celebrate Christ's presence with us now, working in us your new creation. Amen.

(RCD)

Benedictions

1. Go in peace—and take peace—into the world of human need. You are the body of Christ and members of one another. Serve and honor one another, that you may be strengthened to be Christ's body in the world. Amen.

(RCD)

2. Go into the world. You are the body of Christ. God grant you the eyes of Christ to perceive human need, Christ's hands to heal, and Christ's heart to love, through the dynamic energy of the Holy Spirit. Amen.

(RCD)

3. Go forth into the world, rejoicing in the power of the Holy Spirit. Go and join Christ in the world, healing and speaking words of freedom, revealing the sacred in the very midst of life, through the ever-flowing grace of God. Amen.

(RCD)

Lent

An Order of Worship for Ash Wednesday

Greeting

LEADER: Why have we gathered in this place?

PEOPLE: We come in praise of the God of all life and in affirmation of Jesus Christ as the truth and center of our lives. We celebrate places where love is found in life, and we give thanks for the gift of new life that comes to us this lenten season.

Sacrificial Meal

We share together in solidarity with our brothers and sisters in Latin America. *(Food from Latin America is served.)*

General Confession

LEADER: Rend your hearts and not your garments; return to your God.

PEOPLE: For God is merciful and gracious, slow to anger, and abounding in steadfast love.[13]

LEADER: I know well my misdeeds, and my sin is ever before me.

PEOPLE: Wash away my guilt and cleanse me from my sin. [14]

LEADER: Let us ask God to break forth light into the dark places of our hearts and confront us with hidden and secret sins, all that we keep in the dark.

PEOPLE: O God, open our hearts.

LEADER: Our preoccupation with ourselves,

PEOPLE: O God, open our hearts.

LEADER: Our lustful imaginations, our secret ambitions,

PEOPLE: O God, open our hearts.

LEADER: The buried grudge, the half-acknowledged enmity,

PEOPLE: O God, open our hearts.

LEADER: The bitterness of some past loss not yet offered to you,

PEOPLE: O God, open our hearts.

LEADER: The private comforts to which we cling,

PEOPLE: O God, open our hearts.

LEADER: The fear of failure which saps our initiative,

PEOPLE: O God, open our hearts.

LEADER: The pessimism that is an insult to your will and power,

PEOPLE: O God, open our hearts. Here and now, O Holy One, we bring our secret sins to you, we lie open in your sight. Let your piercing light be also our healing, for the sake of Jesus Christ, who both taught us and brought us your forgiveness. Amen.

Sharing of Lenten Reflections

Ceremony of Ashes

Benediction

Join hands for the singing of "Kum Ba Yah."

(WUMC)

Calls to Worship

1. LEADER: This is the season of Lent, a season to remember the sufferings of Jesus Christ.

PEOPLE: A season to remember that to follow Christ is to take up our crosses and to be servants of all.

LEADER: A season to remember Jesus' question "Are you able to drink the cup that I drink?"

PEOPLE: A season to ask ourselves how we, like Simon the Cyrene, might help to bear the cross.

LEADER: A season to ask ourselves how we, like Pilate and Caiaphas and the crowd, continue to nail Christ to the tree.

PEOPLE: A season to ask ourselves how we, like Peter, are afraid and turn away.

LEADER: A season to ask ourselves what we, like the woman with the fine ointment, have to offer.

PEOPLE: A season to give sacrificially to others through the One-Great-Hour-of-Sharing offering.

LEADER: A season to watch and wait with Christ, that we may have courage in the hour of testing.

PEOPLE: A season to proclaim with Mary Magdalene that Christ is not dead but alive!

(MS/RCD)

2. LEADER: In many and various ways, God has spoken of old to our ancestors by the prophets.

PEOPLE: But in these last days, God has spoken to us through Jesus the Christ.

LEADER: We have not a high priest who is unable to sympathize with our weaknesses,

PEOPLE: But one who in every respect has been tempted as we are, yet without sinning.

LEADER: Let us then with confidence draw near to the throne of grace, that we may receive mercy and find grace to help in time of need.

ALL: Let us offer to God acceptable worship, with reverence and awe; for our God is a consuming fire. Amen. [15]

(RCD)

3. *(Transfiguration)*

LEADER: We have gathered as children of God's promise, to keep alive our vision of hope.

PEOPLE: We have gathered on the mountaintop, that we may be strengthened to live as God's children in the valleys of everyday life.

LEADER: We are on a pilgrimage of love and hope.

PEOPLE: We follow the footsteps of Jesus Christ, who was faithful because of God's promise.

ALL: Let us pause on our journeys; let us build a roadside altar, not of stones but of praise, to the God who guides us. Amen.

(RCD)

4. LEADER: We are gathered in the presence of God, who asks us to choose between life and death, blessing and curse.

PEOPLE: We are gathered like the people of Israel, who were challenged to choose the way of life.

LEADER: Like them, we often follow the ways of death.

PEOPLE: Yet, like them, we have the freedom each day to begin anew by the grace of God.

LEADER: By our presence here, we are saying that we want to choose life one more time.

ALL: Let us praise the God of love and life who has called us to this place. Amen.[16]

(RCD)

5. LEADER: It is an awesome thing to stand in the presence of God, to call God's holy name.

PEOPLE: As far as the heavens are above the earth, God's ways are above our ways.

LEADER: But we come with confidence, because in Christ we are called to be God's people.

PEOPLE: Come, let us worship and bow down, let us kneel before God our Maker![17]

(PJF)

6. LEADER: A great teacher once said, "When Jesus Christ calls us, he bids us come and die."[18] We are the people who have responded to this call.

LEFT SIDE: Through Christ, we want to die to the fears that keep us from loving.

RIGHT SIDE: Through Christ, we want to die to the stubbornness that keeps us from sharing our gifts.

LEFT SIDE: Through Christ, we want to die to seeking our own success and salvation in disregard for the good of all God's children.

RIGHT SIDE: This is God's promise, that if we die with Christ, we will also rise with Christ.

ALL: God be praised for the glorious promise of new life in Christ. Alleluia! Amen.

(RCD)

7. LEADER: God calls us away from the tumult of the world, that we may focus our thoughts on things that are lasting.

PEOPLE: In God's presence we see our lives more clearly; the broken pieces are put back together.

LEADER: God calls us out of loneliness into a life of community.

PEOPLE: Worshiping together, caring about one another, we find out what it means to be truly human.

LEADER: But God will send us back into the world's confusion and busyness, its brokenness and isolation.

PEOPLE: We will go with serenity and joy, strengthened to be God's servants, the bearers of peace.

(PJF)

Prayers of Confession

1. Gracious God, we can hardly believe that you have given us life and salvation as a free gift in Jesus Christ! We confess that we continually try to carry the burden of sin and salvation on our own shoulders, rather than trusting your forgiveness and seeking new life in your Spirit. Help us to place our trust in you, and to accept the gift of new life in Jesus Christ. Amen.

(RCD)

2. O God, we confess that we are reluctant to move into this lenten journey to Jerusalem. The past appears pleasant in comparison with the future unknown. We meet pressing human need with fear and pain and inaction. In a chorus with worshipers everywhere, we say, "We have fallen short, we live in a state of brokenness and alienation. We have sinned." O God, our Sustainer and Redeemer, help us to discover the gifts of power, talent, and energy which you give us, that we might bring healing into a broken world. Forgive our sin, strengthen our resolve, and renew us in your ever-vibrant Spirit. Amen.

(WUMC)

3. *(Transfiguration)* God of glory, we confess that we seek to prolong moments of joy and illumination, rather than move on to the dangerous task of being your people in

the real world. Give us courage, that our prayer and praise may be the springboard for living the life to which you call us in Jesus Christ. Amen.

(RCD)

4. Gracious God, you have given us the law of Moses and the teachings of Jesus to direct us in the way of life. You offer us your Holy Spirit, so that we can be born to new life as your children. Yet, O God, we confess that the ways of death have a strong attraction, and that we often succumb to their lure. Give us the vision and courage to choose and nurture life, that we may receive your blessing. Amen.

(RCD)

5. Wise and powerful God, you have given us your light and truth to guide us through confusion, yet we have relied instead on our human wisdom and have lost our way. You offer to share our burdens and give us your strength, yet we trust in our own efforts and find ourselves exhausted. Bring us back into your presence, O God; overcome our separation from one another and from you. By your Word and Spirit, fill us with the gifts that equip us to meet life's demands, that we may be your people in the world and live in the confidence and joy of Jesus Christ, in whose name we pray. Amen.

(PJF)

6. God of truth, how difficult it is for us to be truthful before you. We want to hide our anxieties and fears, our resentments and self-centeredness. Cut through our evasions by the truth of your word, and help us to be honest.

God of mercy, your hopes for us are greater than our own, yet our failures do not surprise you. Forgive us, we pray, even for the sin we cannot see or find it painful to confess.

God of love, accept us as we are, so that we may accept ourselves. Teach us to affirm what is good in our lives, and to put behind us what is unworthy, that by your grace we may live in confidence and joy, in the manner of Jesus our Christ. Amen.

(PJF)

7. O God, our Creator and Sovereign, you have made us to live in freedom and joy before you, in the oneness of love with others. We praise you for the goodness in the world and within us; we seek your help in fulfilling your intentions for us. Sometimes we give our loyalty to other gods. Sometimes we fall into despair or self-pity. Sometimes we separate ourselves from others by our self-centeredness. Fill us with new life, O God, with new joy and new hope, that we may help to make the world more nearly what you want it to be, through Jesus Christ. Amen.

(PJF)

Collective Prayers

1. *(Ash Wednesday)* Most Holy God, before you we feel the limitations of our human power and goodness. Yet we thank you that your forgiveness is as eternal as your righteousness. Teach us never to doubt your love, but always to trust in you, through the grace of Jesus Christ. Amen.

(RCD)

2. *(Temptation)* O God, you know us through and through, you know the many choices we face each day. We choose between right and wrong; we choose between greater and lesser evils; we choose what will be important to us in life. As you strengthened Jesus to choose rightly when he was tempted in the wilderness, so strengthen us, through your presence and Spirit, when we face temptation, that we may walk in the paths most pleasing to you. Amen.

(RCD)

3. Amazing Creator of ourselves and of our world, we thank you that you reveal yourself in the events of human history. We thank you that you have shown yourself in Christ, who shared our human life, walking the path of obedience all the way to the cross.[19] May we also die to ourselves and live for the world, through the empowerment of your Spirit. Amen.

(RCD)

4. *(Cleansing of the Temple)* God of justice and righteousness, deliver us from complacency about our lives and the world in which we live. Drive out from us careless sin. Make us sensitive to all that is sacred; shock us with awareness of any violation of human life in which we participate. May our standard be your Spirit, and not the ways of this world, through the grace of Jesus Christ. Amen.

(RCD)

5. God of grace, Righteous Judge of all people, we thank you that in love you sent Jesus Christ into the world not to condemn, but to save.[20] May your mercy cause us to respond to you in loving commitment, that we may discover the true life you offer us. Amen.

(RCD)

6. *(For One-Great-Hour-of-Sharing Sunday)* Compassionate God, your Christ wept for the people because of the hardness of their hearts. Warm our hearts with your love, so that we might care deeply for the people of our nation and world. Transform our caring into bread for the hungry, healing for the sick, and hope for those who hunger and thirst after justice, to the glory of your name. Amen.

(RCD)

7. Compassionate and all-merciful God, we thank you that in love you sent Jesus Christ to share our earthly life with its joy and suffering. Give us grace, that in our need we may come to you in humility and receive your blessing with open hearts, that we may once again serve you with joy and thanksgiving. Amen.

(RCD)

A Benediction for Lent

LEADER: Go into the world in *faith*!

PEOPLE: Trusting God to lead you, trusting people to receive you.

LEADER: Go into the world with *hope*!

PEOPLE: With God's presence before you and human dreams to carry you.

LEADER: Go into the world with *love*!

PEOPLE: Serving with those in whom Christ lives, and laboring for those for whom Jesus died.

LEADER: Go in Faith, Hope, and Love!

(WRW)

Palm Sunday

Call to Worship

LEADER: Come! From the city streets.

PEOPLE: Join the happy throng that gathers to honor Jesus!

LEADER: Come! From your busy homes and places of business.

PEOPLE: Put down your work in joyful celebration!

LEADER: Come! Lay down your sorrows and worries,

PEOPLE: Turn your eyes toward the Savior whom God has sent!

LEADER: Let all join in joyful song.

PEOPLE: Hosanna! Hosanna! Blessed is Jesus Christ, who comes in God's name. Amen.

(RCD)

Collect

God of infinite power, we praise you for Jesus Christ, who came riding into the city of Jerusalem on a lowly beast, victorious through love and not through violence. Help us to learn the meaning of power and of glory through Christ, who, though being one with you, took on the form of a servant and shared our human life and sufferings. May we truly participate in the life and struggles of the world's peoples, to our joy and your glory. Amen.

(RCD)

Prayer of Confession

God of steadfast love and purpose, you know how we love to serve you in the sunshine of success and popularity, and how we shrink away when you ask us to walk through the fire of trial and suffering! Forgive our unfaithfulness, and teach us to walk with steady obedience in both joy and suffering, through Jesus Christ, your faithful servant. Amen.

(RCD)

Act of Dedication

LEADER: Go forth in celebration.

PEOPLE: Asserting the Presence among us. Christ is here as promised.

LEADER: Go forth in reflectiveness.

PEOPLE: Remembering how quickly we change. We reject tomorrow the one whom we embrace today.

LEADER: Go forth in joy.

PEOPLE: Knowing that God is with us. The suffering is not in vain.

(WUMC)

An Order of Worship for Holy Thursday

Call to Worship

LEADER: You who call upon the name of Christ, we are gathered to recall the story of the night in which Jesus Christ was betrayed. Are you prepared to come to the table of Jesus Christ, whose life was poured out for you?

PEOPLE: By the grace of God, we are.

LEADER: Are you able to watch with Jesus at prayer in the garden, indeed, to struggle yourselves to be in unity with God's will?

PEOPLE: By the grace of God, we are.

LEADER: Will you follow Jesus even into the night of betrayal?

PEOPLE: By the grace of God, we will.

LEADER: Then let us praise God, even in this hour of darkness!

ALL: God of all grace and steadfast love, greatly is your name to be praised in all the earth!

Welcome and Invitation to Communion

Welcome to this service. We will be reenacting tonight the events of Jesus' last night with the disciples. We begin by reenacting the meal Jesus shared with them on that night. As we prepare to come to Christ's table, let us come recognizing who we are.

Unison Prayer of Confession

O Christ, in your presence we discover who we are. You wash our feet, and we learn how reluctant we are to serve one another. Even as you prepare to give yourself for the sake of the world, we are still seeking promotions and possessions. Our love scarcely suffices to fulfill the requirements of good manners, and yet you invite us to eat with you at your table. Forgive us, and help us to value your presence more dearly, that we may find this meal to be a celebration of joy. Amen.

Words of Assurance

Gospel Reading: Luke 22:14-23 or John 13:1-9

Hymn

Sermon

Prayer of Consecration

Creator God, we thank you for bread and for the fruit of the vine. God of freedom, we thank you that you do not leave us in bondage but act in power to liberate us from all oppression. We thank you that Christ, acting in courage and faith, has won for us the victory over sin and death. May the bread and the wine be signs of our renewed covenant with you, and may we ever be faithful, until at last we drink wine anew with Christ in your heavenly realm. Amen.

Distribution of the Elements

Prayer of Thanksgiving

Almighty God, Ruler of the universe, we thank you for your mighty acts of deliverance, when you enable us to cross over from despair to hope, from brokenness to wholeness, from death to life. We thank you for the deep love of Jesus, which moved him to risk himself for the redemption of humanity; and for the grace we experience in receiving these symbols of the life he gave. Through lives given over in commitment to you, make us worthy of this great love. Amen.

With Christ in the Garden of Prayer

Gospel Reading: Luke 22:39-46 or Mark 14:32-42

Call to Prayer

LEADER: Let us join Christ in the garden of prayer.

CONGREGATION: Let us join Christ in passion and victory. [21]

Silence

Pastoral Prayer

O Jesus Christ, Suffering Servant, Lamb of God, we would learn from you the power of trust in God. Your ways seem too hard for us. We fall asleep when we should be praying. We run away when we should be staying. Help us to see what you see and to know what you know. Help us to understand the love of God, so that we can trust the will of God. We hear you say, "O God, if it may be, let this cup pass from me—but if you will, I will drink it." We hear, but we do not understand, and our eyelids close in sleep. Christ, forgive us, and help us to watch with you. Open our eyes so that we can glimpse the reality of God's eternal realm; strengthen our wills, so that in love we may work to make it visible on earth. We are weak, but you can make us strong. Send your Spirit, and hear our prayer, which we pray in your name. Amen.*

Hymn: "'Tis Midnight and on Olive's Brow"

With Christ in the Dark Night of Betrayal

Gospel Reading: Luke 22:47-54a

The Veiling of the Cross

Closing Hymn: "Go to Dark Gethsemane"

Benediction *(Depart in silence)*

(RCD)

---

* Includes allusions to the Seder Service, especially in prayers of consecration and thanksgiving.

NOTE: Some congregations might want to begin the service with a footwashing ritual.

Easter

Calls to Worship

1. LEADER: Oh sing to God a new song.

   PEOPLE: For God has done marvelous things.

   LEADER: Because of God's steadfast love to Israel,

   PEOPLE: All the ends of the earth have seen the victory of our God.

   LEADER: For now is Christ risen from the dead!

   PEOPLE: Make a joyful noise unto God, all the earth.

   LEADER: Break forth into joyous song and praises.

   PEOPLE: For God will rule the earth with righteousness. Nothing in all creation can separate us from the love of God in Jesus our risen Christ. Amen. [22]

           (RCD)

2. LEADER: Now is Christ risen from the dead, and become the firstfruits of them that slept!

   PEOPLE: Break forth into joy, sing together, for God has comforted those whose hearts were broken in sorrow.

   LEADER: Since by human sin came death, so by human faithfulness came resurrection of the dead.

   PEOPLE: Thanks be to God, who gives us the victory through Jesus Christ. Amen. [23]

           (RCD/PJF)

3. LEADER: Springtime changes are bursting forth around us.

   PEOPLE: The earth awakens from winter with a display of wondrous color.

   LEADER: The cycle of living and dying continues.

   PEOPLE: As it has for ages past and will for ages to come.

   LEADER: Lent has passed and the celebration of Easter Sunday is over.

   PEOPLE: But the message of new life, new awakenings, and new possibilities remains with us. Glory to God! Alleluia!

           (WUMC)

4. LEADER: Put away your cares.

   PEOPLE: Put away your anxieties.

LEADER: God has not forsaken us.

PEOPLE: God has not forgotten us.

LEADER: Could a mother forget the child she has nurtured?

PEOPLE: Neither will God forget us.

LEADER: We are imprinted on the palms of God's hands.

PEOPLE: God is with us.

LEADER: God is with us.[24]

(MSG)

5. *(Festival of the Christian Home)*

LEADER: See what love has been given to us, that we should be called children of God.

PEOPLE: By this we know love, that Jesus Christ has come in the flesh, and lived and died, that God's love might be made plain among us.

LEADER: Therefore, beloved, let us not love in word or in speech but in deed and in truth.

PEOPLE: Because we love one another, we know that we have passed from death into life.

ALL: This is the victory that overcomes the world, through Jesus our risen Christ. Amen.[25]

(RCD)

6. LEADER: Come to Christ, that living stone, rejected by the world, but in God's sight chosen and precious.

PEOPLE: We have responded to Christ's call, and seek to be built into a spiritual house, a living reminder[26] of God's presence on earth.

LEADER: Once we were no people, but now we are God's people, called out of the darkness into God's marvelous light. Therefore we sing with the church in all ages:

PEOPLE: Blessed be your name, O God, our Redeemer. By your mercy we have been born anew to a living hope through the resurrection of Jesus Christ from the dead. Amen.[27]

(RCD)

7. LEADER: The Christ said, "This is my commandment: Love one another."

PEOPLE: We come to worship the God who is love, that we may learn to love one another.

LEADER: The Christ said, "No longer do I call you servants; but now I call you my friends."

PEOPLE: We come to worship the God whose friends we are through Christ.

ALL: Let us sing praise to God, and live in love and friendship toward the human family, through Jesus our Christ. Amen. [28]

(RCD)

Prayers of Confession

1. God of birth, God of joy, God of life, we come to you as a people hungry for good news. We have been so dead to miracles that we have missed the world's rebirth. We have preoccupied ourselves with pleasures and have overlooked the joy you offer us. We have been so concerned with making a living that we have missed the Life you set among us. Forgive us, gracious God. Open our eyes and our hearts to receive your gift; open our lips and our hands to share it with all humanity, in the name of our Savior, Jesus Christ. Amen.

(PJF)

2. Almighty and eternal God, we thank you that you have not left us alone in our sin and despair. Loving us, you have brought us good news and set before us the way of Life. Yet we confess that we have failed to see the way. In stubborn pride we have spurned your mercy and your help. In selfishness we have turned away from those who need us. We have allowed ourselves to be crushed by troubles, as though Christ had not been raised at all. Forgive our faithlessness, and grant that we may know new life and hope, in the spirit of the resurrection. In Christ's name we pray. Amen.

(PJF)

3. While the beautiful signs of spring's renewal are revealed by you, O God, we must reveal our failures to bring fresh beauty to many parts of our lives. Like farmers who struggle during the lean months of the year, preparing for a new crop, so we in our life of faith often experience leanness, struggle, and emptiness. We fail to grow, because we do not give ourselves over to the acceptance and nurture possible in this community of your children. Help us to accept responsibility for difficulties in our corporate and personal lives. May we take the risks to open ourselves to you and to one another, and so reap a harvest of love and peace. Amen.

(WUMC)

4. God of endless possibility, we confess that we do not always perceive the opportunities you place before us. Caught up in our own hopes, plans, and fantasies, and crushed when they disappoint us, we are slow to see the open pathways you set before us. Open our eyes, that we may accept the new life you offer us, and thus show forth the resurrection of Jesus Christ. Amen.

(RCD)

5. Gracious Source of Life, we do not always accept the new growth within us. We confess that often we

—do not see the beauty that is in this world for us to enjoy.

—do not recognize the love that is offered to us each day.

—are too busy with our own tasks to see if they fit into God's plan.

—do not want the newfound joy, for then we may no longer pity ourselves.

—are afraid to risk, to turn the corner, to empty the cup, to dance.

Forgive us, O God, and help us to accept your gift of resurrection. Amen.

(WUMC)

6. God of all nations, we praise you that in Christ the barriers that have separated humanity are torn down. Yet we confess our slowness to open our hearts and minds to those of other lands, tongues, and races. Deliver us from the sins of fear and prejudice, that we may move toward the day when all are truly one in Jesus Christ. Amen.

(RCD)

7. O God who labors without ceasing, to bring all people into wholeness and into oneness with you, we confess our reluctance to live in unity with all your people. Help us to overcome the scandal of our pride—the pride of race, creed, class, and color—that your church might be a worthy witness to your good news of love and forgiveness; through Jesus Christ, our risen Head. Amen.

(RCD)

Collective Prayers

1. Gracious God, Power of Life, we praise you that you have not abandoned us to the living death of sin and despair, but that, with Jesus Christ, you have lifted us up from the grave. Grant that we might live in newness of life, that we might ourselves know the power of resurrection, now and in the world to come; for it is in the name of the risen Christ that we pray. Amen.

(RCD)

2. O Source of all living things, we praise you for the power of recurring re-creation of life we see around us, and for the timeless resurrection of Jesus our Christ. May these signs inspire us to manifest your presence in our relationships and actions, that those cries of joy first heard on Easter morning may echo through the centuries to our time and place. Amen.

(RCD)

3. *(Emmaus Road)* O Risen Christ, we are grateful that you walk among us on earth, bringing life and hope. Help us to recognize you; help us to be aware of your presence in our time of worship. Enable us to stand alongside you in your ministry of healing on the crowded roads of our world, through the gift of the Holy Spirit. Amen.

(RCD)

4. *(Festival of the Christian Home)* Parent God, we thank you for the homes in which we were nurtured, and for the love that our mothers and fathers had for us. We thank you also for the new birth that Christ offers us through your love, and for the larger family we find in the church and among the people of the world. Through the power of your Spirit, make us alive to love and serve you in our families, our church, and our world; make us your true children in Jesus Christ. Amen.

(RCD)

5. O living Christ, as the good news of Easter energized your first disciples to establish dynamic Christian communities, so energize us to dynamic life within our congregation. As your Spirit gave them courage to stand tall before the powers of this world, so empower us to proclaim your gospel and struggle for justice and peace.[29] By your presence with us now, make us one in love and mission. Amen.

(RCD)

6. God of grace and glory, we thank you that the life of eternity can be ours in the present, through the resurrection of Jesus Christ. Teach us always to abide in Christ, that we may bear the fruits of love and joy; through the guidance of your Spirit of truth. Amen.

(RCD)

7. We thank you, O God, that Jesus Christ has risen in glory like a bright morning star, to light up the darkness of our lives. May we turn our faces to the sunshine of your love in him, that in our lives we too may reflect your glory. Even so, come quickly, Christ Jesus, and fill us with your Spirit of love and power. Amen.[30]

(RCD)

Resources for Easter Worship with Children or Families

Call to Worship

LEADER: This is a day to celebrate new life,
    To open our ears to the sounds of God's world,
    To open our eyes to the beauty of creation.

PEOPLE: We are glad for green grass and flowers,
    For the music of birds and raindrops.

LEADER: This is a day of gladness and joy;
We remember Jesus, who welcomed all people
And recognized the value of each one.

PEOPLE: We are glad for Jesus,
Our helper and our friend.

LEADER: Jesus is alive! His Spirit lives in us,
helping us when we are afraid
or lonely or ashamed or sad.

PEOPLE: Jesus shows us how much God loves us,
and lets us know we are forgiven.

LEADER: Be glad today. Let's rejoice together.
Life is good. We are accepted and loved.

(LB)

Prayer of Dedication

Thank you, God, for our beautiful cross of flowers. It reminds us that Jesus is alive, helping to make our lives beautiful. Thank you for sharing Jesus with us. Thank you for choosing us to carry on the work Jesus did. We bring our offerings to help in that work. Bless them so that they can do good in our town and all around the world. Help us to be better helpers every day. Amen.

(LB)

Other Resources for the Easter Season

Dedication

LEADER: As Christ was offered in obedience to you, O God,

PEOPLE: So we offer ourselves and our gifts to be used in your service.

LEADER: As you took Christ's sacrifice and filled it with your life and power,

PEOPLE: So use our gifts and transform our lives, that we may be the living presence of your reign on earth, now and always. Amen.

(PJF)

Benedictions

1. LEADER: Now that you have heard the good news, what will you do?

   PEOPLE: We will go out into the world, showing by our lives that Christ is risen indeed!

   LEADER: Praise God! And how will you do this?

   PEOPLE: We will tell the story of God's love for the world in Jesus Christ, and we will continue Christ's loving acts among humanity.

ALL: Alleluia! Praise God! Christ is risen indeed! Amen.

(RCD)

2. LEADER: Let us go forth into the new seasons of our lives.

PEOPLE: We go forth into growing and changing and living.

LEADER: Let us go with caring awareness for the world and all that is in it.

PEOPLE: We go to discover the needs and opportunities around us.

LEADER: Let us go forth in peace and be led out in joy.

ALL: We go in God's continuing presence, with the power to love and the strength to serve. Amen.

(MAN)

3. Go forth into the world, just as God sent Christ into the world. Take with you the peace of Christ, greater than the peace this world gives. And the Spirit will teach you the truth about God, that you may know the joy of Christ in all its fullness. Amen. [31]

(RCD)

4. *(Last Sunday in Eastertide)* Go into the world, with God's new song of love in your hearts. Forgive others, as you are forgiven. Open your hearts to the coming of God's Spirit. And may the peace of God which passes all understanding keep your hearts and minds through Jesus our risen Christ. Amen. [32]

(RCD)

A Call to Worship *(For Yom Hashoah [Day of Remembrance of the Holocaust])*

LEADER: We come to worship the God of compassion, even in the midst of a world where there is much cruelty.

PEOPLE: We gather to proclaim the gospel of Jesus Christ once more, though we are aware that we often lack the courage to speak words of truth and love in daily life.

LEADER: Christ, by your presence among us, give us courage to live as your people day by day.

PEOPLE: We gather as witnesses that God is at work in the midst of human lives, and that love, not cruelty and cowardice, will triumph in the end.

ALL: Glory be to the living God of mercy and compassion, and to Jesus Christ the faithful witness! Amen!

(RCD)

Words of Assurance

LEADER: Jesus said, "I am the vine, and you are the branches. Whoever remains in me will bear much fruit."

PEOPLE: It is God's love that enables us to grow and bear fruit. We say this to one another in faith and confidence, since nothing can separate us from God's love. [33]

(MAN)

Pentecost (and General)

Calls to Worship

1. LEADER: Why have we gathered?

PEOPLE: We have gathered to give witness to the presence of God's Spirit in our time.

LEADER: This Spirit has moved Christ's disciples throughout the centuries to proclaim Christ with a burning desire.

PEOPLE: Christ's disciples were people set on fire by the coming of God's Spirit.

LEADER: We pray for that same Spirit to move among us.

PEOPLE: May it transform that which is hard and dead, and rekindle our faith and action with the flame of Pentecost.

(WUMC)

2. LEADER: A mighty wind has blown,

PEOPLE: And tongues of fire have danced!

LEADER: The presence of the Spirit is with us,

PEOPLE: Just as Jesus the Christ promised.

LEADER: The presence of the Spirit moves and gathers us into community.

PEOPLE: The Spirit moves us to lives of nurturing and challenging one another, celebrating and witnessing.

LEADER: Let us marvel at God's power,

PEOPLE: God's power at work in and through us.

(WUMC)

3. LEADER: Come, let us gather in the awareness of God's love.

PEOPLE: God's love has brought us to this place; it has made of us a church.

LEADER: We can live with confidence and hope, in the assurance that we are forgiven and accepted by a power greater than ourselves.

PEOPLE: Because we are forgiven, we too can forgive.

ALL: Let us praise this God of endless grace, and offer our hearts' true worship. Amen.

(RCD)

4. LEADER: What right have we to invoke God's name on what we say and do here together?

PEOPLE: In Christ we have been called to be God's people, and given God's Spirit and Word.

LEADER: Have we the courage to worship in spirit and in truth, knowing that it may change us?

PEOPLE: We have come to seek, to find, and to be found, with confidence not in ourselves but in God.

(PJF)

5. LEADER: Rejoice, people of God! Celebrate the life within you, and Christ's presence in your midst!

PEOPLE: Our eyes shall be opened! The present will have new meaning, and the future will be bright with hope.

LEADER: Rejoice, people of God! Bow your heads before the One who is our wisdom and our strength.

PEOPLE: We place ourselves before this God, that we may be touched and cleansed by the power of God's Spirit. Amen.

(PJF)

6. LEADER: We are here because we have heard the call of Jesus in our lives.

PEOPLE: We are here to challenge and support one another to rise up and follow.

LEADER: We are here because we want to be God's people.

PEOPLE: We want to learn more about what it means to be the people of God.

LEADER: We come, seeking to be moved, changed, and made whole by the Spirit of the living God.

ALL: Let us open our hearts to the moving of the Spirit, and prepare to leave this place as true disciples of Christ. Amen.

(RCD)

7. LEADER: Let us praise the God who formed the mountains and created the wind.

PEOPLE: Let us sing to the One who made the stars, who turns deep darkness into morning and day into night.

LEADER: Let us turn to God, hating what is evil and loving what is just.

3054

ALL: So may justice roll down like waters, and righteousness like an ever-flowing stream. Amen.[34]

(RCD)

8. LEADER: O God, open us to the powerful winds of your Spirit.

PEOPLE: Open our eyes to the wonders of your creation.

LEADER: Open our nostrils to the smells of life.

PEOPLE: Open our ears to the words of justice and truth.

LEADER: Open our mouths to the taste of freedom and love.

PEOPLE: Open our arms to the touch of our sisters and brothers.

(MB)

9. LEADER: We have been created to be God's children, but we are free to accept or deny this identity.

PEOPLE: We have come to tell the world that we want to live as sons and daughters of God.

LEADER: In Christ, we are called to participate in the life of God. We may come, or stay away.

PEOPLE: We have come to tell the world that Christ is the way, the truth, and the life. Praise be to God!

(PJF)

10. LEADER: We have gathered to rejoice in our oneness in Jesus Christ! Each of us experiences faith and life in a unique way.

PEOPLE: Yet we have one God, one faith, and one baptism, and one Spirit who unites us all.

LEADER: Let us lift our hearts as one, in songs of praise, in prayer, and in listening for God's word.

ALL: Even when we leave this place, let us be joined in common concern for humanity, like that shown by Jesus Christ. Amen.[35]

(RCD)

11. LEADER: Let us open our hearts to the sunshine of God's love.

PEOPLE: Let us open our souls to the gentle wind of God's Spirit.

LEADER: We have gathered to hear the good news of Jesus Christ,

PEOPLE: A Word that renews us again and again.

ALL: Glory be to God, Creator, Christ, and Holy Spirit, who loves, saves, and renews us. Amen.

(RCD)

12. LEADER: God says, "Everyone who thirsts, come to the waters.

    PEOPLE: Come, you who have no money. Come, buy, and eat!"

    LEADER: We have come to feast on the living bread, that we might minister to the world's hungers.

    PEOPLE: We have come to drink from the waters of life, that we might minister to the world's thirst.

    ALL: Blessed are those who hunger and thirst for righteousness, for they shall be filled. Let us worship God, the Source of every blessing. Amen.[36]

    (RCD)

13. LEADER: We have gathered here this morning to worship God.

    PEOPLE: We have come seeking comfort, inspiration, community, and insight.

    LEADER: We have come to open ourselves to the power of God's presence in our midst.

    ALL: We have come to offer up the seasons and the turnings in our lives, and to ask God's help in our learning and in our growing.

    (MAN)

14. LEADER: Now is the time to awaken to the presence of God the Eternal Spirit.

    PEOPLE: Now is the time to come alive with our songs of praise.

    LEADER: Today we open ourselves to the power of the Spirit in our lives.

    PEOPLE: Today we extend our hands in caring toward humanity.

    ALL: We do all this because we have responded to the ministry and message of Jesus Christ, whose people we are.

    (RCD)

15. LEADER: Oh come, let us worship and bow down, let us kneel before God our Maker.

    PEOPLE: We come in humility, opening ourselves to God's wisdom and strength.

    LEADER: We are the people of God's pasture and the sheep of God's hand.

    PEOPLE: We come with expectation, that in God's presence we may know ourselves and one another, and be truly at home in the world.[37]

    (MAN)

16. LEADER: We are the community of faith that has been created by the love of God.

    PEOPLE: We are the people who have been set free by the word of forgiveness in Jesus Christ.

LEADER: We have come not to parade our own goodness but to praise the holiness of God.

PEOPLE: We have come not to boast of what we have done but to proclaim the redeeming work of Jesus Christ.

ALL: With all our being, we will praise you, O God, and tell of all your kindness toward us. Amen.

(RCD)

17. LEADER: As shepherd seeks a lost sheep,

PEOPLE: So God seeks and saves the lost.

LEADER: Like a woman who searches for a lost coin until it is found,

PEOPLE: So God rejoices over one soul restored to wholeness.

LEADER: As a father receives a returning wayward son,

PEOPLE: So God welcomes us, and lets the past be the past.

LEADER: Therefore let us praise God in thanksgiving that we are received.

PEOPLE: Let us receive and welcome and rejoice over one another in the name of Jesus Christ. Amen.

(RCD)

18. LEADER: We have come to worship God. Let us come with humility.

PEOPLE: We offer all that we are, knowing that we need God's Spirit to be what we ought to be.

LEADER: We have come to worship God. Let us come with expectation.

PEOPLE: In the Divine Presence there is light for our darkness and purpose in our striving. Praise be to God!

(PJF)

19. LEADER: We are gathered to give witness to the enduring realities of life.

PEOPLE: We have come to affirm that life is a gift, that the gift is good, and that it comes from God.

LEADER: We are gathered to renew our hope in Jesus Christ, as we travel life's long journey.

PEOPLE: We find God in the paths of our present and our past, but we also trust in God's love in our future.

LEADER: The same God guides us all the way, every day of our lives, and beyond life.

ALL: Let us praise God with our whole hearts, and entrust our lives to God's hands. Amen.

(RCD)

20. LEADER: Rejoice in our God always!

PEOPLE: Again I say rejoice!

LEADER: For God has gathered us together

PEOPLE: From all the corners of the earth,

LEADER: To be present now,

PEOPLE: And to know the joyful unity

LEADER: Of being one with Christ.

PEOPLE: Rejoice in our God always!

LEADER: Again I say rejoice.[38]

(MSG)

21. LEADER: O Holy One, you are our God.

PEOPLE: We will exalt you, we will praise your name.

LEADER: For you have done wonderful things—

PEOPLE: Plans formed of old, faithful and sure.

LEADER: You have been a stronghold to the poor,

PEOPLE: A stronghold to the needy in distress.

LEADER: You subdue the noise of violence and hatred,

PEOPLE: As the shade of a cloud subdues the heat.

LEADER: O Holy One, you are God.

PEOPLE: We exalt you, we praise your loving name.[39]

(RS)

22. LEADER: And these are the words of God:

PEOPLE: I will go before you and level the mountains;

LEADER: I will give you the treasures of darkness,

PEOPLE: That you may know

LEADER: That it is I, the God of Israel, who call you by your name.

PEOPLE: I call you by your name.

LEADER: I am God, and there is no other.

PEOPLE: From the rising of the sun and from the west,

LEADER: I am God, and there is no other.

ALL: Let us worship God together.[40]

(MSG)

23. LEADER: A new day has dawned.
God's gift of life is renewed in you and me.

PEOPLE: Praise God for today!
Praise God for the creative spirit in our midst.

LEADER: Be still and know that God is here.
Let the Spirit in.

PEOPLE: We are ready to pray and think and rejoice.
We are ready to hear God's word.

LEADER: Then listen and respond to God, who meets us in new ways and in different sounds, today in worship, and every day in the world.

PEOPLE: Come to us, O God, and guide our worship. Speak. Speak to us the Word we need, and let that Word change us and empower us to be your people. Amen.

(LB)

24. *(Reformation or All Saints)*

LEADER: We have come to affirm our historic faith.

PEOPLE: To worship the God of our mothers and fathers.

LEADER: We have come to remember God's benefits to us the living.

PEOPLE: To respond in thanksgiving to the mighty works of God in our lives.

LEADER: We have come to affirm our trust in the God of all futures,

PEOPLE: To whose name be blessing and honor, glory and power forever and ever. Amen.

(RCD)

25. *(A Call to Worship for Communion Sunday)*

LEADER: On this day we gather in oneness with our brothers and sisters to celebrate God's gifts.

PEOPLE: We hear the call to rekindle our spirits and to receive strength for our common tasks.

LEADER:	On this day we will share the bread and wine, which are symbols of God's power and love.
PEOPLE:	We will open our hearts to accept these gifts, seeking the grace to walk in God's ways.

(MAN)

26. LEADER: As Jesus of Nazareth came to Bethany in Judea, come, O Christ, to us today.

PEOPLE: May you find here with us, O Christ, as sincere a welcome as you found among your friends so long ago.

LEADER: May we be as eager as Mary to sit at your feet and learn from you.

PEOPLE: May our faith be as strong and sure as Martha's when she declared Jesus to be the Christ, the Resurrection, and the Life.

LEADER: May we, like Lazarus, find new life in you.

PEOPLE: And may we learn to show our gratitude in ways as plain as she who anointed you with costly ointment.

LEADER: Let us worship God.

(MS)

Prayers of Confession

1. LITURGIST: The Spirit calls each of us.

PEOPLE: But we are often reluctant to heed the call. The wind of the Spirit blows, at times fiercely, and draws us onward. Yet we cling to the fragile familiarities, to securities, and to safety. Help us to risk letting go, to stand free as your servant people. Help us to capture visions of the future, so that we can truly be the church. We ask this in the name of Jesus the Christ. Amen.

(WUMC)

2. O Christ, if we carry the name Christian, we are signs of your presence. Yet we confess that we sometimes hurt people through our pride, rather than showing the way to the healing waters of your Spirit. When we are discouraged ourselves, we are unable to be signs of joy or hope or good news. Forgive us, and give us grace to be earthly reminders of your love. Amen.

(RCD)

3. O God, you have spoken to men and women of old through dreams and visions, yet we confess that we seek to rely on reason and tradition alone. Fill us with vision, lead us into the future, and enable us to grow toward a deeper understanding of your nature, through the power of your Holy Spirit. Amen.

(RCD)

4. O Life that surges through all living things and is their Source, we confess that we have often closed ourselves off and prevented the river flow of life through us. We have lost touch with the unique worth of the life each of us has to live. Our eyes fail to perceive beauty in people and in the world. Open our eyes, that we may walk in newness of life through One who is the Resurrection and the Life. Amen.

(RCD)

5. Most loving God, we can scarcely comprehend the scope of your forgiveness, we can hardly believe your amazing care for us. We confess that often we close ourselves off from your saving presence; and in our pride, we withhold forgiveness from other people. Through the power of your Holy Spirit, grant us the assurance of your love. May our hearts be filled with gratitude for your grace which overflows with love toward others. Amen.

(RCD)

6. We come into your presence with thanks, Creator God, for all that fills our lives with joy: the love of family and friends, the comfort of our homes, the challenge of work, and the delight of leisure. Forgive us that too often we have taken all these for granted, failing to see them as your gifts. In this time of worship, stretch our understanding, that we may know our lives in the perspective of your sovereign authority. Teach us to live in the world with faithfulness to your intention for the world, and to be at home wherever your spirit leads us; through Jesus Christ your faithful witness. Amen.

(PJF)

7. Almighty God, you have called us into your church to be your servants in the service of others.[41] Forgive us for falling short of your call. We have loved our buildings more than our brothers and sisters. We have been more concerned with budgets than with justice and peace. We have been more ready to talk about Christ than to live in Christ's image. Cut through our evasions, increase our courage, renew our vision. Make us and the whole church more nearly what you would have us be; through Jesus Christ, whose Body we are. Amen.

(PJF)

8. Most gracious God, Giver of life, who loves and forgives us though unworthy, we confess that we are burdened by excess baggage as we travel the roads you send us down. We are caught up too soon in the trappings of religion, rather than rejoicing in the life of the Spirit. We seek too quickly to be a successful organization rather than a church on a mission. Too often we wish to be served rather than to serve. For all this, forgive us, and free us to walk the paths of righteousness; through Jesus Christ the Way. Amen.

(RCD)

9. We give thanks, merciful God, that in Christ you seek to unite all things in heaven and in earth, and to reconcile all people to one another and to you. Yes, we confess that the new creation is not yet complete in us, and that we feel everywhere the

barriers that separate humankind. Forgive us, and fill us with your Spirit of oneness. Reveal to us those places where pride and selfishness rebuild the walls once torn down in Christ; through the power of your Spirit. Amen. [42]

(RCD)

10. Dear God, for the day you have given us, with all its possibilities, we thank you. For your gifts of life and love, of labor and rest, we praise your holy name. Forgive us that too often we are unappreciative while your goodness surrounds us; that we feel alone when there are many who love us; that we despair when your strength is near at hand. Tear down the walls that isolate us, make strong the ties that bind us, and help us to walk together with joy in all your ways; through the grace of Jesus Christ and the power of your Spirit. Amen.

(PJF)

11. O most gracious God, we confess that we spend much of our lives on that which does not satisfy. [43] We do not always count our time and resources as precious gifts, but squander them in meaningless activities and seemingly urgent needs. Look kindly upon us, for the temptation to waste is overwhelming in our world. Enable us to understand what is important, and to use the gifts of life responsibly, for we want to be your people in word and in deed. Amen.

Words of Assurance

The good news is that God forgives us and gives us Christ to be living water and true bread. [44] Let us accept with joy these precious gifts of abundant life. Amen.

(RCD)

12. O God, we come into your presence confessing our sin and our indifference to the sin and suffering of our world. Our lives are fragmented with mundane concerns: paying bills, washing diapers, shuffling papers, buying groceries, typing letters, chauffering children, studying, and sleeping. We are easily overwhelmed by considerations of students dying in Cape Town, political prisoners suffering in Chile, people struggling for a just society in Zimbabwe, and for survival in the urban ghettos of our land. We come into your presence admitting our humanness, yet emboldened by the knowledge that we stand before the Ruler of all peoples, who continues to call us to join in the struggle for justice, peace, and liberation, personal and corporate, here and around the globe. Strengthen our resolve, and free us to be fully human with our brothers and sisters on the planet earth; in the name of Jesus Christ the Liberator. Amen.

(WUMC)

13. Almighty and merciful God, we confess that as we come into the presence of Christ and one another, we are unprepared in heart and mind. We bring with us cherished hurts and angers; we fail to receive one another as sisters and brothers. Yet we come trusting in your grace and forgiveness. By your Spirit, awaken in us the

freshness of new life, and give us wisdom to make differences of opinion or background an occasion for learning. Amen.

(RCD)

14. Author of life, we humbly confess that too often we fall short of your intentions for us and of our expectations of ourselves.

We would touch the world with goodness, but often we withdraw in anxiety and self-concern.

We would live with integrity and stand for truth, but we are torn with uncertainties.

We would warm the lives of others with our love, but we hesitate, wondering if they will love us in return.

We would go about our daily tasks with confidence and joy, but find ourselves struggling with self-doubt.

We need your presence, O God, if we are to be what we could be and want to be. Let our worship heal us, renew us, strengthen us, that we may go out in joy and be led forth in peace. Amen.

(PJF)

15. Creator God, we confess that we do not give our lives over to the transforming power of your Spirit to call out the gifts of each one of us and to build up the life of the whole church. Today as we wonder at your creation in the world around us, may we also open ourselves to the new creation you seek to bring about within and among us, through the grace of Jesus Christ. Amen.

(RCD)

16. O God, Source of all that makes life possible, Giver of all that makes life good, we gather to give you our thanks. Yet we confess that we have often failed to live our thankfulness: What we have we take for granted, and we grumble about what we lack. We have squandered your bounty with little thought for those who will come after us. We are more troubled by the few who have more than we than by the many who have less. Forgive us, O God. In this hour of worship, accept our thanksgiving, and teach us to make gratitude and sharing our way of life; through the grace of Jesus Christ. Amen.

(PJF)

17. Righteous God, we live in a world where human life is exploited and abused. Violence is taken lightly, and people are often viewed as objects. Images of hunger and war and murder flash before us until we become nearly hardened. If we have taken on these values of the world, forgive us. Give us tender hearts, help us to reflect your righteousness, and give us courage to challenge the wrongs we see; through the power of the Holy Spirit. Amen.

(RCD)

18. Before you, O God, we must confess how fragile is our spirit of cooperation with the many churches of Christ. In our eagerness to be a vital, active congregation, we become jealous of signs of life in other churches. Any uncertainty we have about our faith tempts us to ridicule the faith of others. We compare ourselves to other congregations, forgetting the unique strengths and resources you have given us for the mission of Christ. Help us to shed all these comparisons and jealousies and to keep alive the vision of oneness in Christ, whom we all serve; through the unifying power of your Spirit. Amen.

(RCD)

19. Gracious Giver of all that we have and are, we confess that each of us is slow to give thanks and to share. Sometimes we deny our oneness with all your creatures, and seek only after our own salvation, our own needs and hopes. Challenge us with a vision for all people, that we may commit our lives to your mission in the world; for we are yours. Amen.

(RCD)

20. O God of Grace, we confess that sometimes we are unsure of our faith. We are weighed down with doubt and guilt, and do not have the courage to trust in you. Fill our hearts with the assurance of your love, and renew our courage through your Holy Spirit, that we may serve you with joyful abandon. Amen.

(RCD)

Collective Prayers

1. Most Holy God, we await the touch of your Spirit with eagerness. We ask that you enter the lives of each one of us today, refreshing and renewing and healing us with the power of your loving Spirit, that we may live with purpose and enthusiasm and courage after the manner of Jesus, who was truly whole. Amen.

(RCD)

2. Tender and compassionate God, whose strength is made perfect in our weakness, help us to believe that you receive us as we are. More than that, help us, imperfect though we are, to be carriers of the message of your love, like earthen vessels that carry treasures; and may we worship you in spirit and in truth, through the grace of Jesus Christ. Amen.[45]

(RCD)

3. O God of amazing grace and miraculous power, we are secular people in a secular world. Our prayer is like that of one who said so many years ago, "I believe; help my unbelief."[46] We have difficulty believing the miracles of scripture, but even more difficulty trusting your ability to work through us today. Be gentle with us, O God, in our slowness to believe; increase our faith, and make us alive through your Spirit of hope and power. Amen.

(RCD)

4. Amazing God, you have shaped the world in wonder and mystery. With thanks we contemplate the good earth you have created and the joys of the senses. With awe we contemplate the unseen world, with its divine and demonic realities. You have created us so that we live as citizens of worlds seen and unseen. Help us, your creatures, to live so that your Spirit may become visible in our actions and relationships; through the grace of Jesus Christ, who shared our earthly life. Amen.

(RCD)

5. God of tenderness, we thank you that you care for us individually and intimately. We thank you that you know us through and through and yet love us. Jesus said that the hairs of our heads are numbered and that you care even for the sparrows. [47] As you are aware of our needs, so awaken us to the needs of others, that we may respond in concern. Amen.

(RCD)

6. Eternal Giver, as we thank you for the wondrous, precious gift of life, we are aware of how time slips through our fingers. Caught up in yesterday's dreams and tomorrow's hopes, we pass by the opportunities of today. Grant us courage to meet the challenges of today motivated by the vision of your reign, which is coming into being every moment. Amen.

(RCD)

7. O God, in mystery and silence you are present in our lives, bringing new life out of destruction, hope out of despair, growth out of difficulty. We thank you that you do not leave us alone but labor to make us whole. Help us to perceive your unseen hand in the unfolding of our lives, and to attend to the gentle guidance of your Spirit, that we may know the joy you give your people. Amen.

(RCD)

8. O God, before you our lives and intentions are plain. What do you see when you see our hearts? Does the Word you speak to us fall on rocky ground or among weeds? [48] Or have we become simple, open, and willing in our faith? Send your Spirit to fill our lives with your love, that we may not only hear but also do your Word. Amen.

(RCD)

9. Eternal God, who created all things from the void, teach us to know the power of silence and of prayer. Fill our emptiness with your peace and your love, and fill our darkness with your light. Fulfill in us the potentials for which we were born and were called into your church, for we pray in the name of Jesus Christ, who sought your presence even in the rush of life. Amen.

(RCD)

10. O God, you are the Source of our life. It was you who mysteriously knit us in our mother's wombs. It was you who nurtured us through the love of family and friends, and through your own mysterious outpouring of affection. You form us, O God, and

you break us apart, that we might return to you. You are the beginning and the end. Be with us this day, O God, as we seek to understand more clearly our call to be loving, just, and fully human. Amen.

(MB)

11. O God of life, there is much that deals in doubt and despair and death in our world, and we are often tempted to succumb to these forces. Help us always to choose life; to affirm what can be affirmed, to hope where hope is possible; and to risk ourselves to lift up human dignity. For we pray in the name of Christ, who is the way and the truth and the life. Amen.

(RCD)

12. O God of love and power, we have seen your mighty works in the world and in our own lives. Yet like the disciples who witnessed the feeding of the multitude, but were afraid when they saw Jesus walking on the sea, our faith must be renewed day by day, hour by hour. Renew us with your Holy Spirit, that we may trust you, and that we may act in trust, even as Peter walked out to meet Christ on the water. Amen.[49]

(RCD)

13. Creator God, we place ourselves before you as children eager to learn of your marvelous works. Breathe into us the refreshment of your Word, as we once again recall our sacred history. Make pliable our clay, that we might creatively meet the future. Tickle our being, that we might be totally present in this moment. Keep our hearts pounding and our veins surging with the blood of new life. Recall for us that we are children of your love. Amen.

(MB)

14. Gracious God, we give thanks for the gospel record and for the simple words Jesus spoke, which help us understand your presence in the world and the coming of your reign. Help us to understand Jesus' words, and to see the signs and parables you have for us in the world today; through the power of your Spirit. Amen.

(RCD)

15. O God of love, you have called us into the church. We thank you for opportunities to grow in understanding and concern for one another. May our congregation be an incarnation of your love within and beyond these church doors, wherever there is loneliness, injustice, or misunderstanding; through Christ our Head, and the Holy Spirit our Strength. Amen.

(RCD)

16. Most compassionate God, we thank you that you have come to us in Jesus Christ, sharing our common lot.[50] As the shepherd seeks a lost sheep, you seek us when we wander; finding us, you receive us with rejoicing. Since you have claimed us, fill us with your Spirit, that we might be channels of your tender care for those who are brokenhearted or wandering. Amen.

(RCD)

17. O God, you receive us when we turn to you; you heal us through the power of forgiveness. Through your Spirit, enable us to show our gratitude by forgiving others. Deliver us from secret jealousy and desire for revenge, so that we may live in peace with you and with our human brothers and sisters. Amen.

(RCD)

18. Eternal God, we long for truths that are lasting, yet we want our faith to be alive to the people and problems of today. As we sail forward in an ever-changing world, may faith in Christ be our anchor, and your love be our guide, through the presence and power of the Spirit. Amen.

(RCD)

19. O God of steadfast love, we thank you for the lessons of the past. We remember all that you have done for us; make us truly thankful. We remember times of joy and sorrow; may these experiences make us compassionate toward others. We share the memory of your people as they have journeyed through time; it is our story as well. May the richness of our past be the ground out of which love, hope, and faithfulness blossom; through the grace of Jesus Christ. Amen.

(RCD)

20. Gracious God, we thank you for all the good things with which you fill our lives, but most of all for the vision of peace and justice and freedom in Christ that draws us into the future. May we be your people in the world, in word and in deed, in spirit and in truth. Grant that we may not be play-actors, but people who show we truly care, like Jesus Christ, whose life was love. Amen.

(RCD)

21. Bounteous God, you have offered us the fullness of life in Christ; you have invited us to the feast of rejoicing. We thank you that you seek us out on the roadways of life, before we even ask. Clothe us in righteousness so that we may be worthy guests at your table. Amen.

(RCD)

22. Almighty God, whose eternal rule is ever present but always beyond us, claim our lives. Give us grace to live as your children in this world, which does not yet fully honor you or your Christ, yet where your Spirit is powerfully at work; through Jesus Christ, the first pioneer of your righteous realm. Amen.

(RCD)

23. O Christ, Living Bread, from the world with its abundance which does not satisfy our hunger, we turn to you. O Christ, Living Water, from the world with its floods which do not satisfy our thirst, we turn to you. Gather up the broken fragments of our lives and make us whole again, that we may live to your glory, and not draw back in times of testing. Amen.

(RCD)

24. Eternal Source of all life, be with us this day as we seek to open ourselves to your love and your wholeness. Fill us with your compassionate spirit, so that we can serve the whole world into which we are called. Help us recall that it is your breath that flows through us—your breath of creative love. Let us affirm your love, your life, and your work, amid our everyday world of electric can-openers and car wax, transportation strikes and picnics. Help us to remember that love and justice are not words in the Bible on the shelf, but a kind of life we are called to live this day. Amen.

(MB)

25. Eternal Source of life, be with us this day as we seek to open ourselves to your love and your wholeness. Be with us as we set aside our everyday worries and concerns and concentrate on your forgiveness and loving-kindness. Create in us anew a sense of meaning and purpose, in the Spirit of the Christ. Amen.

(MB)

Special Resources for Pentecost

A Litany of Corporate Confession

LEADER: The breath of the Spirit does not abandon us, though sometimes we choose the rush of other winds.

PEOPLE: In the winds of trade and academics, the winds of fortune or poverty, the winds of controversy and activism, the winds of anxiety and despair, we forget why we are and whose we are.

LEADER: Our confusion keeps us from recognizing the Spirit that blows within each of us and spreads to all—often because we do not expect that Spirit.

PEOPLE: It seems easier to extinguish a spark than to give ourselves to the transforming fire, as witnesses for a new order.

LEADER: The Spirit of what is holy incites us to witness.

PEOPLE: But accepting the challenge of seeking and acting sometimes seems too hard for us in our weakness.

LEADER: The Spirit fuses us in loving community with energies to empower our world.

PEOPLE: But we tire of setting priorities, of being effective, of being intentional about the work God calls us to do in the world. Where is the Spirit's wind and fire then?

LEADER: Let us lift up our individual joys and sorrows, successes and defeats, as an act of accountability for our lives and the life of our world, and as an act of awareness of the presence of the Spirit's wind and fire in all of life.

PEOPLE: May God be with us,

LEADER: And with our spirits.

PEOPLE: Let us pray. *(A time of free prayer follows, ending with the prayer Jesus taught his disciples. Let the community respond to each prayer with an Amen.)*

LEADER: By faith and grace we know that whenever we get together again we will be refreshed by the Spirit moving with us, and by God's Word given to us in Jesus Christ. Within this hope, we move forward to the future again, affirming the Christ in ourselves and in each other.

(WUMC)

Liturgical Resources for the Season of the New Earth*

A Litany of Confession

LEADER: Tilling difficult soils and planting new seeds often makes us feel uncomfortable and vulnerable, and sometimes we are afraid.

PEOPLE: Wherever we labor, it seems too hard to break new ground, and too easy to lose sight of the harvest.

LEADER: We shy away from conceiving of our work relationships . . . in banks, in classrooms, in hospital wards, in offices, in homes, and in restaurants . . . as sites for the New Earth; we need to be more imaginative about the possibilities.

PEOPLE: Even if we succeed in the plantings, we grow weary and impatient waiting for luxuriant growth. We use "megatools" when hoes would do, or we bog down making frantic repairs and modifications when new instruments are required.

LEADER: We are unwilling to see that if we are to create a society of vital communities—free of injustice and inequality, and peopled by empowered, participating citizens—we must stop laboring by ourselves, for ourselves.

PEOPLE: It is hard for us to forge a commitment to join one another in identifying New Earths, in seeking and using only the most appropriate tools and technologies, in being wise about resources and in being determined to create just relationships. We fear the loss of ourselves in the doing.

LEADER: Because we have felt God's presence among us, we are confident that our joys are received, and that even in our hesitant weariness our spirits will be revitalized. Refreshed by the good news of the Christ, we rejoice in the creative tension between ourselves and other members of our communal body. We look forward to joining with God in enabling one another to labor compassionately, to seek for the New Earth, and to have the love and patience to nurture new life. We are glad that we share both the sowing and the reaping. And we thank God that we don't have to do it alone.

ALL: Amen!

(WUMC)

---

* Called Kingdomtide in some traditions; celebrated as part of Pentecost in others.

A Call to Awareness

LEADER: Welcome to our celebration of New Earth, the season when the church focuses on the world into which it was sent as a transforming presence. We are the seeking people, drawn together from all the places where we are working in the world.

PEOPLE: As we gather to worship God and to nurture one another, we seek to be aware of the connection between our faith commitment and our daily lives.

LEADER: Let us consider what is required for the biblical model of equity and justice to be fulfilled in society's institutions.

PEOPLE: We open ourselves to innovative visions of God's new earth, and we joyously join together to celebrate Christ's presence among us.

LEADER: Amen!

ALL: Amen!

(WUMC)

Prayer of Confession

There have been times when we've felt scattered about, disjointed, dried up, all our energy gone. There have been times when we've been out of joint with your Spirit, unable to move, dead, lifeless. Not trusting in your forgiveness or your power, we trust only in ourselves, and our lives become dry and brittle. Fill us with your Spirit, O God, that we may be transformed. May what was dead, scattered, and disjointed become alive, like the bones of Ezekiel's vision, that we may be one body in Christ, equipped to be your people in the world. Amen.

(WUMC)

The Sending Forth

LEADER: The Spirit of God is upon us.

PEOPLE: God has anointed us to bear good news to the afflicted,

RIGHT: To bind up the broken hearted,

LEFT: To proclaim freedom to the captives,

ALL: To open the prisons of those who are bound. Amen and amen.

LEADER: Greet one another with the Shalom of Jesus the Christ, who seeks peace in broken relationships, who seeks healing in alienated persons, who seeks justice in oppressive structures. Share this shalom by saying, "May the peace of Christ be yours today."

(WUMC)

Benedictions for Pentecost

Go into the world, shouting through your lives the self-giving love of Jesus Christ, who became poor for our sakes. Through the power of the Spirit and the love of God, may you serve others as though serving Christ. Amen.

(RCD)

LEADER: As Jesus sent the disciples out into the countryside to preach and to heal, so Christ sends us out to speak words of hope and to heal human hurts today.

PEOPLE: We accept this mission to be God's people in the world.

LEADER: Go on your way, rejoicing in the presence of God's Spirit, and in the power of the gospel of love and hope.

ALL: For yours is the glory, O God, now and forever! Amen.

(RCD)

Let us now depart and hold fast to the Covenant, knowing that in Christ we are no longer strangers and sojourners but dearly loved children of the living God.

(MSG)

As we leave this place, know that God loves us and has called us to be a blessing in the midst of the earth. Go in peace, knowing that the new covenant of right relationship with humanity, with God, and with the earth resides within your heart and motivates your every action. Amen.

(MB)

Affirmation of Faith (for Pentecost)

We believe in God, the Creator Spirit,
    who moved upon the face of the deep at the beginning of creation,
    who created all that is,
    and who spoke through the prophets of old.

We believe in Jesus Christ,
    into whom God's Spirit was poured in fullness and in power,[51]
    that the whole creation might be restored and unified;
    and who promised that the Spirit would come
    and fill the faithful with power to witness
    to the mighty love of God.

We wait on that Spirit today with longing hearts,
    seeking to be empowered to witness to God's love in Christ,
    with fresh words and courageous actions of love and hope.

Glory be to God—Creator, Christ, and Holy Spirit—
    now and always. Amen.

(RCD)

Prayer of Dedication (After Communion)

Eternal God, having shared in your sacred covenant-renewing meal, let us now also share in your sacred work on earth. As we have received sustenance for our bodies, minds, and spirits, may we share our transformed selves with other persons and families in our local and global communities.

Alienation, separation, and sin are conquered by your love. We are forgiven; we are energized to bring your reconciling message of wholeness into the world. We dedicate our lives to your service, through One who came to model a life of service. Amen.

(MB)

Anywhere Along the Road: Resources for Any Time

Resources Based on the United Church of Christ Statement of Faith

Calls to Worship

1. LEADER: We are here not because we have found God but because God our Creator has called us here,

   PEOPLE: Challenging us to accept the cost and joy of discipleship, and to be servants in the service of the whole human family.

   LEADER: But the call is also God's promise:

   PEOPLE: A promise of forgiveness of sins and fullness of grace, courage in the struggle for justice and peace, and eternal life in that realm which has no end.

   ALL: Blessing and honor and glory and power be unto God!

   (PJF/RCD)

2. LEADER: Come, let us praise God, who promises us forgiveness of sins and fullness of grace.

   PEOPLE: Let us praise Christ, who is present with us in trial and rejoicing.

   LEADER: Let us praise the Spirit, who encourages us in the struggle for justice and peace.

   ALL: We sing together in thanksgiving to the one God, with the church throughout time! Amen.

   (RCD)

3. LEADER: Why have you gathered here?

   PEOPLE: We have responded to the gospel of God's love for us in Jesus Christ.

   LEADER: What do you hope to do here?

   PEOPLE: We hope to be united with the faithful of all ages, tongues, and races in praising the God of love and power.

   LEADER: With what mission will you be sent from this place?

   PEOPLE: To be God's servants in serving humanity, to spread the gospel, and to resist the powers of evil.

ALL: Let us then draw near to God, who promises to forgive us, to fill us with courage, and to be present with us in this world and in the world to come. Amen.

(RCD)

4. LEADER: We have come to celebrate the presence of Jesus our Christ,

PEOPLE: Whom we recognize as we join in the breaking of bread.

LEADER: We gather through the grace of the Holy Spirit, who creates and renews the church of Jesus Christ.

PEOPLE: Binding in covenant faithful people of all ages, tongues, and races, with whom we lift our song of praise:

ALL: Holy, Holy, Holy, One God Almighty, Your glory fills all the heavens and the earth!

(RCD)

A Benediction

God sends us into the world, to accept the cost and to discover the joy of discipleship. Therefore go—carrying with you the peace of Christ, the love of God, and the encouragement of the Holy Spirit, in trial and rejoicing. Amen.

(RCD)

Prayers and Litanies

A Litany: God's Call to Life

Preparation

LITURGIST: All life is a call and a response. God calls us into creation. God calls us into life. How we live is our response to God. As we share in this call to awareness, let your response be "God calls me to this day," and raise your arms as a sign of your response. God calls us to Life! God calls each of us to move among the creations of this world and bring joy and renewing love. God calls us this day.

COMMUNITY: God calls me this day!

LITURGIST: God calls us to Love, to plunge ourselves into the hurts and the horrors, to give ourselves fully to those who are in need. God calls us to be present to those who are without love. God calls us this day.

COMMUNITY: God calls me this day!

LITURGIST: God calls us to dance, to move out our joy and sadness, shedding our self-consciousness and clothing ourselves with peace. No longer can we afford to wait. We are builders of the Body of Christ. God calls us this day!

COMMUNITY: God calls me today!

LITURGIST: In God we live, move, and have our being.[1]

COMMUNITY: Amen.

LITURGIST: We've all received the unexpected in life.

COMMUNITY: We receive and extend many invitations, spoken and unspoken, in need and in friendship. Our loneliness is that we do not hear or accept these invitations from one another. Instead, we live as if we must carry the weight of the whole world on our shoulders. Bills are due, opportunities pass by, and life seems to be breaking up right and left all around us. We trudge through life in meaningless circles, never breaking free, never sharing our burdens. We are guilty of looking only at ourselves. We must rise out of that darkness, that aloneness. Each of us can leave that old path of life and respond to the call to dance. Each of us has been called.

Silent Time
Affirmation

LEFT: Rise, for God has come among us.

RIGHT: Rise, for you are part of God's loving creation.

LEFT: Rise, for Christ has taken your burden.

RIGHT: Rise, for you are not alone in the world.

(WUMC)

A Litany of Confession

LEADER: In our confession today, we are not confessing things for which we need to feel personally guilty or individually responsible. Rather, we are acknowledging what life is often like in an imperfect world. Our confession this morning is a responsive one. I will make a statement, and then you will respond with "That's how it is."

LEADER: We find ourselves separated from our sisters and brothers.

RESPONSE: That's how it is.

71

LEADER: There are lines drawn between us that are racial, that are economic. *(Response)*

LEADER: We live cut off from many sources of strength and power, and often feel that we cannot act. *(Response)*

LEADER: So many things call to us, grab for our attention, that we find ourselves stretched to a fine, thin line. *(Response)*

LEADER: Our time is fragmented, our lives are fragmented. We are broken. *(Response)*

LEADER: Yet in the face of all this, we seek out the dawning of our liberation. *(Response)*

ALL: O God, our liberation, that's how it is with our lives. We seek the power of your Spirit, that we may live in fuller union with you and our sisters and brothers, and that we may gain courage to love and to act. Amen.

(MSG)

A Litany of Dedication

PASTOR: The Creator of all life and love has endowed our earth with bountiful blessings.

PEOPLE: God has created humanity to share in the wonder and joy of these blessings.

PASTOR: All thanks be to God, Giver and Receiver of all that is good.

PEOPLE: We return to God portions of what God has given us: our time, the fruits of our labors, our commitment.

PASTOR: May the giving from the fullness of our lives be acceptable in God's sight.

PEOPLE: May the gifts we bring prove God's Rule is at hand—both now and to come.

PASTOR: God calls us to participate in the construction of a New Reality. We now dedicate these, our offerings, toward the enrichment of our life as a covenant community, and toward the ministry God has given us.

PEOPLE: We dedicate our labors, our time, and our commitment to God, who calls us into discipleship and who surrounds us and sustains us with Everlasting Love.

ALL: Praise God from whom all blessings flow!

(MB)

A Litany of Faith and Courage

LEADER: O God of Abraham and Sarah, you have led your people in the past; lead us now.

PEOPLE: Grant us the courage of Ruth to leave behind the old and familiar, the courage of Noah to risk laughter and scorn, the hope of Jeremiah to invest in the future, and the unselfishness of Esther to take risks on behalf of others.

LEADER: O God of Moses and Miriam, you delivered your people and led them through the wilderness, giving them food, protection, and guidance.

PEOPLE: In the words of Miriam, we praise you: "I will sing to Yahweh, who has triumphed gloriously!"[2]

LEADER: O God of Deborah and Gideon, you have given us leaders to bring us back when we wander from you, and deliverers to lead us against oppression.

PEOPLE: Give us leaders and deliverers, and grant us the wisdom to follow them.

LEADER: From the words of your prophets we have learned justice and mercy.

PEOPLE: Help us to say, with Isaiah, "Here am I. Send me."[3]

LEADER: O God of James and John and Mary Magdalene, you have called us to follow Jesus.

PEOPLE: Teach us how to work together in mutual responsibility, side-by-side, neither tagging behind nor shoving to the front.

LEADER: O God of Paul and Priscilla and Aquila, who risked their lives for the sake of spreading your church, fill us with enthusiasm for your church.

PEOPLE: Use us in the spreading of the church, in the building up of its parts, in the joining together of its various congregations, and in ministry to the whole world.

LEADER: O God of our Lord Jesus Christ, who gave himself in love for the whole world, teach us so to love.

PEOPLE: Grant us the spirit of Christ, who came not to be served but to serve. Amen.

(MS)

Prayer of Commitment

LEADER: O God, we are persons, each of us.

PEOPLE: We stand alone in history, yet there are others, only a hand's length away, with whom we could join our spirits, to bring into being a soul-force that might spread to many and transform us all.

LEADER:	Make us aware, O God, of the pain of the world.
PEOPLE:	Help us to hear the cry of the oppressed,
LEADER:	The poor,
PEOPLE:	The prisoners.
LEADER:	Make us aware, O God, of the joys of life.
PEOPLE:	Help us to hear the beauty of the earth,
LEADER:	Of people,
PEOPLE:	Of ourselves.
LEADER:	O God, help us to listen.
PEOPLE:	For in listening, we will speak our love,
LEADER:	And by listening
PEOPLE:	We will be moved to act in faith.

(MSG/RS)

A Litany of God's Love

LEADER:	Whatever we may have to go through now is less than nothing compared with the magnificent future in store for us.
PEOPLE:	The whole of creation is on tiptoe to see the wonderful sight of the daughters and sons of God coming into their own.
LEADER:	If God is for us, who can be against us?
PEOPLE:	The Great Spirit who does not hesitate to be manifest in human form—can we not trust such a Presence to give us everything we need?
LEADER:	Can anything separate us from the love of Christ? Can trouble, pain, or persecution?
PEOPLE:	Can lack of clothes and food, danger to life and limb, the threat of force of arms?
LEADER:	No, in all these things we win an overwhelming victory through One whose love for us has been proved.
ALL:	I have become absolutely convinced that neither death nor life, neither messenger of heaven nor ruler on earth, neither what happens today nor what may happen tomorrow, neither power from on high nor power from below, nor anything else in God's whole world has any power to separate us from the love of God! Amen![4]

(MSG)

A Litany: The Word Became Flesh

LEADER: In the beginning was the Word, God's self-disclosure.

PEOPLE: The Word was with God,

LEADER: As the energy that brought all things into being.

PEOPLE: The light embodied in that Word was the light of the human race.

LEADER: A light that shines in darkness.

PEOPLE: A light that darkness has not overcome.

LEADER: A prophet came, whose name was John.

PEOPLE: John came as a witness,

LEADER: As a witness to bear testimony to the light.

PEOPLE: For the Word, the true light that enlightens all people, was coming into the world.

LEADER: Many of God's own people were blind to its shining.

PEOPLE: But all who were able to perceive the light were given power to become the children of God.

LEADER: Yes, all who believe in the One whose power to save came not from human characteristics, not maleness, or Jewishness, or anything human,

PEOPLE: But from God alone.

LEADER: And this is the wonder: that *the Word became flesh* in one Jesus of Nazareth,

PEOPLE: And, wonder of wonders, even we, late in time, have been transformed by God's glory shining in Christ, full of grace and truth!

ALL: Blessing and honor and glory and power be unto the God who has come to us, and spoken to us, in flesh, in blood, in this very human form, the Word of truth and light for all ever! Amen.[5]

(RCD)

A Litany of New Birth

LITURGIST: O gracious God of life and birth,

CONGREGATION: How you labor, how you suffer, to bring forth the new creation!

LITURGIST: Indeed, you cry out like a woman in childbirth.

CONGREGATION: And the Spirit groans with you.

LITURGIST: But your cries become cries of joy,

CONGREGATION: As you behold fragile new life there before you.

LITURGIST: All creation waits on tiptoe for the revealing of your daughters and sons;

CONGREGATION: We ourselves long to take part in the glorious liberty of your children.

LITURGIST: Who can separate us from the love of God?

CONGREGATION: Even a mother might forget us,

LITURGIST: Yet you will not forsake us!

CONGREGATION: O God, our God, how wonderful is your name in all the earth! [6]

(RCD)

Songs for the Journey:
Responsive Psalms

Psalm 4

Answer me when I call to you, O God, my justice.

You have received me in the past when I was in distress.

Be gracious with me, and hear my prayer.
Tell me, children of earth, how long will I suffer disgrace?

How long will you love empty words and delight in lies?

Know that the godly belong to God alone.

Yahweh hears my cry for help.

Be angry, but do not sin.

Look to your own hearts on your beds, and be silent.

Make sacred your gifts to God;

Place your trust in Yahweh.

Many say, "Oh, that better days would come;

"Shine on us with the light of your presence, O God."

As for me, I remember the joy you have already put in my heart, greater than the joy they have when their barns are full of grain, and their veins are full of wine.

In peace, I will lie down and sleep, for in your care alone, O God, I rest secure.

(RCD[1])

Psalm 8

O God, our God, how majestic is your name in all the earth!

Your glory above the heavens is chanted by the mouths of babes and infants.

You have founded a bulwark because of your foes,

To still the enemy and the avenger.

When I look at the heavens, the work of your fingers, the moon and the stars which you have established;

What is humanity that you are aware of us, and our children that you care for them?

Yet you have made us little less than yourself, and crowned us with glory and honor.

You have given humanity dominion over the works of your hands;

You have put all things under our feet,

All sheep and oxen, and also the beasts of the field,

The birds of the air, and the fish of the sea, whatever passes along the paths of the sea.

O God, our God, how majestic is your name in all the earth!

(MB[2])

Psalm 16 (vv. 1-4a, 5-9, 11)

Preserve me, O God, for in you I take refuge.

My soul sings out: "You are my God; I have no good apart from you."

As for the saints in the land, they are the noble, in whom is all my delight.

Those who follow another god multiply their sorrows; the Holy One is my chosen portion and my cup: You hold my destiny. The lot you have measured for me is pleasant; yes, I have a goodly heritage.

I bless you, for you give me counsel; in the night also my heart instructs me.

I have set you always before me; because you are at my right hand, I shall not be moved.

Therefore my heart is glad, and my soul rejoices; my body also dwells secure.

You show me the path of life; in your presence there is fullness of joy, in your right hand are pleasures forever.

(WGM[3])

Psalm 25 (vv. 1-2, 4-12, 14, 21)

To you, O God, I lift up my soul.

O my God, in you I trust, let me not be put to shame; let not my enemies exult over me.

Make your ways known to me, O God; teach me your paths.

Lead me in your truth, and teach me, for you are the God of my salvation; for you I wait all the day long.

Be mindful of your mercy, O God, and of your steadfast love, for they have been from of old.

Remember not the sins of my youth, or my transgressions; according to your constant love remember me, for your goodness' sake, O God.

You are good and upright; you instruct sinners in the way.

You lead the meek in what is right, and teach the humble your way.

All your paths are steadfast love and faithfulness, for those who keep your covenant and testimonies.

For your name's sake, O God, pardon my guilt, for it is great.

Is there one who fears God?

Such a person God will teach the way that is right.

Your friendship is for those who fear you; to them the covenant is made known.

May integrity and uprightness preserve me, for I wait for you.

(WGM)

Psalm 32 (vv. 1-8, 10-11)

Blessed is the one whose transgression is forgiven, whose sin is covered.

Blessed is the person to whom God imputes no iniquity, and in whose spirit there is no deceit.

When I did not declare my sin, my body wasted away through my groaning all day long.

For day and night your hand was heavy upon me; my strength was dried up as by the heat of summer.

I acknowledged my sin to you, and I did not hide my iniquity;

I said, "I will confess my transgressions to God"; then you forgave the guilt of my sin.

Therefore let everyone who is godly offer prayer to you;

At a time of distress, in the rush of great waters, they shall not reach you.

You are a hiding place for me, you preserve me from trouble; you encompass me with deliverance.

I will instruct you and teach you the way you should go; I will counsel you with my eye upon you.

Many are the pangs of the wicked; but steadfast love surrounds the one who trusts in God.

Be glad in God, and rejoice, O righteous, and shout for joy, all you upright in heart!

(WGM)

Psalm 33

Rejoice in God, O you righteous! Praise befits the upright.

Praise God with the lyre, make melody with the harp!

Sing to God a new song, play skillfully on the strings, with loud shouts.

For the word of God is upright; the work of the Most High is done in faithfulness.

God loves righteousness and justice; the earth is full of the covenant loyalty of God.

By the word of God the heavens were made, and all their host by the breath of God's mouth.

God gathered the waters of the sea as in a bottle, placing the deeps in storehouses.

Let all the earth fear God, let all the inhabitants of the world stand in awe of our God!

For God spoke, and it came to be; God commanded, and it stood forth.

God brings the counsel of the nations to nought: God frustrates the plans of the peoples.

The counsel of God stands forever, the thoughts of God's heart to all generations.

Blessed is the nation whose God is Yahweh, the people whom God has chosen as a heritage!

God looks down from heaven, and sees all the children of humanity;

Enthroned above them all, God looks forth on all the inhabitants of the earth,

God who fashions the hearts of them all, and observes all their deeds.

A ruler is not saved by a great army; a warrior is not delivered by great strength.

The war horse is a vain hope for victory, and by its great might it cannot save.

Behold, the eye of God is on those who fear God, on those who hope in covenant loyalty.

That God may deliver their souls from death, and keep them alive in famine.

Our soul waits for God, our help and shield.

Yea, our heart is glad in God, whose holy name we trust.

Let your covenant loyalty, O God, be upon us, even as we hope in you.

(MB)

Psalm 46

God is our refuge and strength, a very present help in trouble. Therefore we will not fear, though the earth should change, though the mountains shake in the heart of the sea; though its waters roar and foam, though the mountains tremble in its tumult.

The God of hosts is with us; the God of Jacob and Rachel is our refuge.

There is a river whose streams make glad the city of God, the holy habitation of the Most High. God is in its midst, the city shall not be moved; God will help the city right early. The nations rage, the dominions totter; God utters a word, the earth melts.

The God of hosts is with us; the God of Jacob and Rachel is our refuge.

Come, behold the works of God bringing desolation in the earth. God makes wars cease to the end of the earth, breaks the bow, shatters the spear, and burns the chariots with fire! "Be still, and know that I am God; I am exalted among the nations, I am exalted in the earth!"

The God of hosts is with us; the God of Jacob and Rachel is our refuge.

(MB)

Psalm 57 (vv. 1-3, 5, 7, 9-11)

Be merciful to me, O God, be merciful to me, for in you my soul takes refuge;

In the shadow of your wings I will take refuge, till the storms of destruction pass by.

I cry to God Most High, to God who upholds me.

God will send from heaven and save me, sending forth steadfast love and faithfulness!

Be exalted, O God, above the heavens! Let your glory be over all the earth!

My heart is steadfast, O God, my heart is steadfast! I will sing and make melody!

I will give thanks to you, O God, among the peoples; I will sing praises to you among the nations.

For your steadfast love is great to the heavens, your faithfulness to the clouds.

Be exalted, O God, above the heavens!

Let your glory be over all the earth!

(WGM)

Psalm 62 (vv. 1-2, 5-8, 11b-12)

In silence my soul waits for God, who alone is my salvation.

God only is my rock and my salvation, my fortress; I shall not be greatly moved.

In silence my soul waits for God, who alone is my hope.

God only is my rock and my salvation, my fortress; I shall not be shaken.

My deliverance and my honor rest on God, who is my mighty rock, and my refuge.

Trust in God at all times, O people; pour out your heart before God; God is a refuge for us.

All power belongs to you, O God; and to you, O God, belongs steadfast love;

For you reward your people as their work deserves.

(WGM)

Psalm 65 (vv. 1-9a, 9c-11a, 12b-13)

Praise is due to you, O God, in Zion; and to you shall vows be performed, to you who hears prayer!

To you shall all flesh come on account of sins. When our transgressions prevail over us, you forgive them.

Blessed is the one whom you choose and bring near, to dwell in your courts!

We shall be satisfied with the goodness of your house, your holy temple!

By dread deeds you answer us with deliverance, O God of our salvation, the hope of all the ends of the earth, and of the farthest seas;

By your strength you have established the mountains, for you are girded with might;

You still the roaring of the seas, the roaring of their waves, the tumult of the peoples, so that those who dwell at earth's farthest bounds are afraid at your signs;

You make the outgoings of the morning and the evening to shout for joy.

You visit the earth and water it; you greatly enrich it; you provide grain, for so you have prepared it.

You water its furrows abundantly, settling its ridges, softening it with showers, and blessing its growth.

You crown the year with your bounty; the hills gird themselves with joy, the meadows clothe themselves with flocks,

The valleys deck themselves with grain; they shout and sing together for joy.

(WGM)

Psalm 69 (vv. 1-3, 13-17, 30-34)

Save me, O God! For the waters have come up to my neck. I sink in deep mire, where there is no foothold; I have come into deep waters, and the flood sweeps over me.

I am weary with my crying; my throat is parched. My eyes grow dim with waiting for my God.

My prayer is to you, O God. At an acceptable time, O God, in the abundance of your steadfast love answer me.

With your faithful help, rescue me from sinking in the mire. Let me be delivered from my enemies and from the deep waters. Let not the flood sweep over me, or the deep swallow me up, or the pit close its mouth over me.

Answer me, O God, for your steadfast love is good; according to your abundant mercy, turn to me. Hide not your face from your servant; for I am in distress, make haste to answer me.

I will praise the name of God with a song. I will magnify God with thanksgiving. This will please God more than an ox or a bull with horns and hoofs.

Let the oppressed see it and be glad; you who seek God, let your hearts revive. For God hears the needy, and does not despise those that are in bonds.

(MB)

Psalm 74 (vv. 12-17, 19-21)

God my Sovereign is from of old, working salvation in the midst of the earth.

You divided the sea by your might; you broke the heads of the dragons on the waters.

You crushed the heads of Leviathan, you gave him as food for the creatures of the wilderness.

You cleaved open springs and brooks; you dried up ever-flowing streams.

Yours is the day, yours also the night; you have established the luminaries and the sun.

You have fixed all the bounds of the earth; you have made summer and winter.

Do not deliver the soul of your dove to the wild beasts; do not forget the life of your poor forever.

Have regard for your covenant; for the dark places of the land are full of the habitations of violence.

Let not the downtrodden be put to shame; let the poor and needy praise your name.

(MB)

Psalm 77 (vv. 1-8, 11-14, 16-20)

I cry aloud to God, aloud to God that I may be heard.

In the day of trouble I seek God; in the night my hand is stretched out without wearying; my soul refuses to be comforted.

I think of God, and I moan; I meditate, and my spirit faints.

You hold my eyelids from closing: I am so troubled that I cannot speak.

I consider the days of old, I remember the years long ago.

I commune with my heart in the night; I meditate and search my spirit: "Will God spurn forever, and never again be favorable? Has God's steadfast love forever ceased? Are God's promises at an end for all time?"

I will call to mind the deeds of God; yea, I will remember your wonders of old.

I will meditate on all your work, and muse on your mighty deeds.

Your way, O God, is holy. What god is great like our God?

You are the God who works wonders, who has manifested your might among the peoples.

When the waters saw you, O God, when the waters saw you, they were afraid, yea, the deep trembled.

The clouds poured out waters; the skies gave forth thunder; your arrows flashed on every side.

The crash of your thunder was in the whirlwind; your lightnings lit up the world; the earth trembled and shook.

Your way was through the sea, your path through the great waters; yet your footprints were unseen.

You led your people like a flock, by the hand of Moses, Miriam, and Aaron.

(MB)

Psalm 91 (vv. 1-12, 15-16)

Those who dwell in the secret place of the Most High, who abide in the shadow of the Almighty, will say, "My refuge and my fortress, my God, in you I trust."

For God will deliver you from the snare of the fowler and from the deadly pestilence; under the feathers of God's wings you will find refuge.

God's faithfulness is a shield and buckler. You will not fear the terror of the night, nor the arrow that flies by day, nor the pestilence that stalks in darkness, nor the destruction that wastes at noonday.

A thousand may fall at your side, ten thousand at your right hand; but it will not come near to you. You will only look with your eyes and see the recompense of the wicked.

Because you have made God your refuge, the Most High your habitation, no evil shall befall you, no scourge come near your tent.

For God will give angels charge of you to guard you in all your ways. On their hands they will bear you up, lest you dash your foot against a stone.

When my child calls to me, I will answer; I will be there in trouble, I will provide rescue and give honor.

With long life I will give satisfaction and show my salvation.

(WGM)

Psalm 93

God reigns, robed in majesty; the Almighty is robed, girded with strength. The world is established; it shall never be moved; your throne is established from of old; you are from everlasting.

The floods have lifted up, O God, the floods have lifted up their voice, the floods lift up their roaring.

Mightier than the thunders of many waters, mightier than the waves of the sea, the Most High is mighty!

Your decrees are very sure; holiness befits your house, O God, forevermore.

(WGM)

Psalm 95 *(in unison)*

O come, let us sing to God; let us make a joyful noise to the rock of our salvation!

Let us come into God's presence with thanksgiving; let us make a joyful noise with songs of praise!

For God is a great God, and a great sovereign above all gods.

In God's hand are the depths of the earth, and the heights of the mountains also.

The sea belongs to God, its Maker, whose hands formed the dry land.

O come, let us worship and bow down, let us kneel before God, our Maker!

For we are of God. We are the people of God's pasture, and the sheep of God's hand.

(MB)

Psalm 96

O sing to God a new song;

Sing praise, all the earth!

Sing, and bless God's name; tell of God's salvation from day to day.

Declare God's glory among the nations, and marvelous works among all peoples!

For great is God, and greatly to be praised; God is to be feared above all gods.

For all the gods of the people are idols: but our God made the heavens.

Honor and majesty are before God; strength and beauty are in God's sanctuary.

Ascribe to God, O families of the peoples, ascribe to God glory and strength!

Ascribe to God the name of glory; bring an offering, and come into the courts divine!

Worship God in holy array; tremble in awe, all the earth!

Say among the nations, "God reigns!

Yea, the world is established, it shall never be moved; God will judge the peoples with equity."

Let the heavens be glad, and let the earth rejoice;

Let the sea roar, and all that fills it;

Let the field exult, and everything in it!

Then shall all the trees of the wood sing for joy before God,

For God comes to judge the earth.

God will judge the world with righteousness, and the peoples with truth.

(MB)

Psalm 97 (vv. 1-5, 10-12)

God reigns; let the earth rejoice; let the many coastlands be glad!

Clouds and thick darkness are round about God; righteousness and justice are the foundation of God's throne.

Fire goes before God, and burns up adversaries round about.

God's lightnings light up the world; the earth sees and trembles.

The mountains melt like wax before God, before the God of all the earth.

God loves those who hate evil; God preserves the lives of the saints; God delivers them from the hand of the wicked.

Light dawns for the righteous, and joy for the upright of heart.

Rejoice in God, O you righteous, and give thanks to God's holy name!

(MB)

Psalm 102 (vv. 1-2, 11-12, 18-22, 25-27)

Hear my prayer, O God; let my cry come to you! Do not hide your face from me in the day of my distress!

Incline your ear to me; answer me speedily in the day when I call!

My days are like an evening shadow; I wither away like grass.

But you, Most High, are enthroned forever; your name endures to all generations.

Let this be recorded for a generation to come, so that a people yet unborn may praise you:

That God looked down from holiness above, from heaven regarding the earth, to hear the groans of the prisoners, to set free those who were doomed to die;

That your name may be declared in Zion, that you may be praised in Jerusalem, when peoples and nations gather together to worship you.

Of old you laid the foundation of the earth, and the heavens are the work of your hands.

They will perish, but you endure; they will all wear out like a garment.

You change them like raiment, and they pass away; but you are the same, and your years have no end.

(WGM)

Psalm 113

Praise Yahweh! Praise, O servants of Yahweh, praise the name of God.

Blessed be the name of God from this time forth and for evermore!

From the rising of the sun to its setting, the name of God is to be praised!

Yahweh is high above all nations, with glory above the heavens!

Who is like Yahweh our God, who is seated on high, who looks far down upon the heavens and the earth?

God raises the poor from the dust, and lifts the needy from the ash heap, to make them sit with nobility, with the nobility of the people.

God gives the barren woman a home, making her the joyous mother of children.

Praise Yahweh!

(MB)

Psalm 116 (vv. 1-9, 12-14, 17, 19b)

I love Yahweh, the God who has heard my voice and my pleading.

As long as I live, I will call upon Yahweh, whose ear was inclined to me.

Death surrounded me like snares;

The pangs of hell held me in their grip;

I suffered anguish and distress;

Then I called upon Yahweh by name.

I said, "Yahweh, I beg you, save my life!"

Our God is gracious, good and compassionate, rescuing the simple.

When I was at rock bottom, it was God who saved me.

Return, O my soul, and rest, for God has dealt bountifully with you.

For you, O God, have delivered my soul from death,

My eyes from tears,

My feet from stumbling.

I walk before you now in the land of the living.

What shall I offer to you, O God, for all your goodness to me?

I will lift up the cup of salvation and call upon your name.

I will pay my vows to you in the presence of all your people.

I will offer to you, O God, the sacrifice of thanksgiving, and call upon your name as long as I live. Praise Yahweh!

(RCD)

Psalm 131

O God, my heart is not lifted up,

My eyes are not raised too high.

I do not occupy myself with things too great and too marvelous for me.

But I have calmed and quieted my soul, like a child quieted at its mother's breast:

Like a child I am quieted in my soul.

Let us all hope in God, now and forever.

(MB/RCD)

Psalm 139

O God, you have searched me and known me!

You know when I sit down and when I rise up; you discern my thoughts from afar.

You search out my path and my lying down, and are acquainted with all my ways.

Even before a word is on my tongue, O God, you know it completely.

You beset me behind and before, and lay your hand upon me.

Such knowledge is too wonderful for me; it is high, I cannot attain it.

Where shall I go from your Spirit? Or where shall I flee from your presence?

If I ascend to heaven, you are there! If I make my bed in Sheol, you are there!

If I take the wings of the morning and dwell in the outermost parts of the sea,

Even there your hand shall lead me, and your right hand shall hold me.

If I say, "Let only darkness cover me, and the light about me be night,"

Even the darkness is not dark to you; the night is as bright as the day, for darkness is as light with you.

How precious to me are your thoughts, O God! How vast is the sum of them!

If I would count them, they are more than the sand. When I awake, I am still with you.

Search me, O God, and know my heart! Try me, and know my thoughts!

See if there be any wicked way in me, and lead me in the way everlasting!

(MB)

Psalm 144 (vv. 3-9, 12-15)

O God, what is humanity that you regard us, or our children that you think of them?

We are like a breath, our days are like a passing shadow.

Bow your heavens, O God, and come down! Touch the mountains that they smoke!

Flash forth the lightning and scatter them, send out your arrows and rout them!

Stretch forth your hand from on high, rescue us and deliver us from the many waters, from the hand of aliens, whose mouths speak lies, and whose right hand is a right hand of falsehood.

I will sing a new song to you, O God; upon a ten-stringed harp I will play to you.

May our children in their youth be like plants full grown, our daughters like corner pillars cut for the structure of a palace; may our garners be full, providing all manner of store; may our sheep bring forth thousands in our fields; may our cattle be heavy with young, suffering no mischance or failure in bearing; may there be no cry of distress in our streets!

Happy the people to whom such blessings fall! Happy the people whose God is Yahweh!

(MB)

Psalm 146

Praise Yahweh! Praise Yahweh, O my soul! I will praise Yahweh as long as I live; I will sing praises to my God while I have being.

Put not your trust in earthly rulers, in human beings, in whom there is no help. When their breath departs they return to the earth; on that very day their plans perish.

Happy are those whose help is the God of our forebearers, whose hope is in Yahweh their God, who made heaven and earth, the sea, and all that is in them; who keeps faith forever; who executes justice for the oppressed; who gives food to the hungry.

Yahweh sets the prisoners free; Yahweh opens the eyes of the blind.

Yahweh lifts up those who are bowed down; Yahweh loves the righteous.

Yahweh watches over the sojourners and upholds the powerless; but the way of the wicked is brought to ruin.

Yahweh will reign forever, your God, O Zion, to all generations!

(MB)

Psalm 147

Praise Yahweh! For it is good to sing praises to our God, who is gracious; a song of praise is seemly.

Yahweh builds up Jerusalem, gathering the outcasts of Israel.

God heals the brokenhearted, and binds up their wounds.

God determines the number of the stars, giving to all of them their names.

Great is our Yahweh, and abundant in power; God's understanding is beyond measure.

Yahweh lifts up the downtrodden, casting the wicked to the ground.

Sing to Yahweh with thanksgiving; make melody to our God upon the lyre!

God covers the heavens with clouds, prepares rain for the earth, makes grass grow upon the hills.

God gives to the beasts their food, and to the young ravens which cry.

God does not take delight in the strength of a horse, or in the muscles of humans; God takes pleasure in those who hope in God's steadfast love.

Praise Yahweh, O Jerusalem! Praise your God, O Zion! For God strengthens the bars of your gates and blesses your children within you.

God makes peace in your borders and fills you with the finest wheat.

God sends forth a command to the earth; God's word runs swiftly.

God gives snow like wool, scattering hoarfrost like ashes.

God casts forth ice like morsels; who can stand before such cold?

God sends forth the word, and melts them, making the wind blow and the waters flow.

God declares the word to the children, the statutes and ordinances to the nation.

Praise Yahweh!

(MB)

Notes

Mile-Markers: Resources for the Sacraments and Rites of the Church

1. See Joshua 24:15.
2. Paraphrase of Joshua 24:16-17.
3. Based on Revelation 1:4-6.
4. See Revelation 3:15-16.
5. See Revelation 2:10.
6. Paraphrase of Revelation 5:30.
7. Paraphrase of Revelation 4:11.
8. Paraphrase of Revelation 4:8.
9. Paraphrase of Revelation 5:9-10.
10. Paraphrase of Revelation 5:12.
11. See Revelation 22:16.
12. Paraphrase of Revelation 11:17.
13. Based on the *Te Deum laudamus*.
14. From the eucharistic prayer in the *Didache*.
15. See Mark 9:24.
16. See Isaiah 53:3.
17. Hebrews 12:1.

Time-Markers: Resources for the Church Year

1. See Luke 1:46-47.
2. Quotes Psalm 96:11, 13.
3. See Isaiah 35:1-10.
4. See Colossians 1:19, 20.
5. See Colossians 3:15-16, TEV.
6. See 1 Corinthians 1:18-30.
7. See Luke 2:36-38 and Zechariah 9:9.
8. See John 1:14.
9. Written by Charles Bagby for the 1978 Annual Meeting of the United Church of Christ Board for World Ministries.
10. Paraphrase of Psalm 57:7-11.
11. Paraphrase of Isaiah 56:1, 6-7.
12. See Matthew 5:3-10.
13. Paraphrase of Joel 2:13.
14. Paraphrase of Psalm 51:3.
15. Includes paraphrases of Hebrews 1:1-2, 4:15-16, and 12:28-29.
16. With allusions to Deuteronomy 30:15-20 and Joshua 24:14-28.
17. Includes paraphrases of Isaiah 55:9 and Psalm 95:6.
18. Dietrich Bonhoeffer, *The Cost of Discipleship* (New York: Macmillan, 1967).
19. See Philippians 2:8, TEV.
20. See John 3:17.
21. An allusion to the Statement of Faith of the United Church of Christ. (See inside back cover of *Everflowing Streams*).
22. Based on Psalm 98:1, 3, 4 and Romans 8:39.
23. Quotes of 1 Corinthians 15:20 (KJV) and paraphrases Isaiah 52:9 (KJV) and 1 Corinthians 15:21, 57.
24. Paraphrases Isaiah 49:14-18.
25. Includes paraphrases and quotations from 1 John 3:1, 14, 16, 18; 5:4.
26. See Henri J. Nouwen, *The Living Reminder: Service and Prayer in Memory of Jesus Christ* (New York: Seabury Press, 1977).
27. Paraphrases and quotes 1 Peter 1:3 and 2:4-10.

28. Paraphrases John 15:12-15.

29. An allusion to the Statement of Faith of the United Church of Christ.

30. See Revelation 22:16, 20.

31. See John 14.

32. Paraphrases Philippians 4:7.

33. Includes paraphrase of John 15:5.

34. Based on Amos 4:13; 5:8, 15, 24.

35. Based on Ephesians 4:1-6.

36. Paraphrases Isaiah 55:1 and quotes Matthew 5:6.

37. Paraphrases Psalm 95:6-7.

38. Paraphrases Philippians 4:4.

39. Paraphrases Isaiah 25:1-5.

40. Quotes and paraphrases Isaiah 45:1-6.

41. An allusion to the Statement of Faith of the United Church of Christ.

42. See Ephesians 1:10 and 2:14.

43. See Isaiah 55:2.

44. See John 4:7-15 and 6:35-40.

45. Based on 2 Corinthians 12:9 and 4:7.

46. Mark 9:24.

47. Luke 12:6-7.

48. See Matthew 13:1-17.

49. Based on Matthew 14:22-29 and 15:32-38.

50. An allusion to the Statement of Faith of the United Church of Christ.

51. See Colossians 1:19-20.

Anywhere Along the Road: Resources for Any Time

1. See Acts 17:28.

2. Includes paraphrase of Exodus 15:1.

3. Isaiah 6:8.

4. Based on paraphrase of Romans 8:18-19, 31-32, 35, 38-39 as translated by J. B. Phillips, *The New Testament in Modern English* (New York: Macmillan, 1958). Used by permission.

5. Based on John 1:1-14.

6. Based on the following passages: Romans 8:19 (PHILLIPS), 21, 22, 35; Isaiah 49:14-15. This litany is here reprinted with slight changes from "Expanding Our Language About Humanity," copyright © 1977, Office for Church Life and Leadership, United Church of Christ. Used by permission.

Songs for the Journey: Responsive Psalms

1. Psalms acknowledged as RCD were paraphrased by Ruth C. Duck, using the *Revised Standard Version of the Bible* as a basis.

2. Psalms acknowledged as MB were paraphrased by Michael Bausch with reference to the *Revised Standard Version of the Bible* and to the psalms in Hebrew.

3. Psalms acknowledged as WGM were paraphrased by William George Myers, O.S.L., using the *Revised Standard Version of the Bible*. For Psalms 16 and 91, the *King James Version* was also used.